"I have had the privilege to live such a unique life playing loud rock 'n' roll and touring the world for over two decades. Since I invited Christ to live inside of me and live His life through me He has connected me with His most passionate followers all around the world. I can honestly say that out of every passionate group of people I've met, my friends at Steiger are at the top of the list.

In *Jesus in the Secular World: Reaching a Culture in Crisis*, Ben Pierce shares with us that very passion that he and everyone at Steiger walks in.

I'm going to ask everyone that reads his book not to read it like any other book. I highly recommend reading *Jesus in the Secular World* slow. Drink in the spirit of what Ben is sharing, and be born again with a new level of passion for Christ that you've never had before!"

Brian "Head" Welch
- Co-founder of the band Korn and New York Times best-selling author of 'Save Me From Myself,' as well as 'Stronger' and 'With My Eyes Wide Open.'

"Ben Pierce is a remarkable person with an infectious love for Jesus that motivates him to love people like Jesus did. Writing out of life experience, Pierce shows that a generation of people inclined toward sarcasm, contempt or apathy toward Jesus can winsomely be invited to fall in love with him. By reading this book, you'll be challenged - challenged to pray like never before, challenged to courageously tell others why you love Jesus, and challenged to go beyond your comfort zone to places where lost people live. I encourage you to join Ben and his family on this journey."

Jay Barnes
- President, Bethel University (Saint Paul, Minnesota - USA)

"Defying our categories of missionary focus, the growing globalization youth movement is presenting an entirely new "tribe" for the church to engage. We must sharpen the tools of contextualization, deep cultural understanding, language learning, and incarnational ministry, to love these people into the Kingdom. Ben Pierce lays out the challenges of this tribe, while showing how the church can walk through the holes that secularism is burning in the hearts of these precious people."

Ted Esler
- President of Missio Nexus

"Let's face it, we live in an upside-down world where right is considered wrong, and wrong is said to be right. The mainstream media and prevailing secular culture are becoming increasingly hostile towards the Church and regrettably, our response is often to isolate ourselves from the very world that our Lord has called us into. Through his dissection of the Scripture and personal anecdotes, my good friend Ben shows us how to creatively and tactfully infiltrate the world with the best news of all—the Gospel. *Jesus in the Secular World* will show you how to bridge the gap and be "In this world, but not of the world," without losing your saltiness or your relevance. Highly recommend!"

Mark Mohr
- Lead vocalist of the Billboard chart-topping Gospel Reggae group, Christafari

"Many people think we are losing the next generation but Ben Pierce believes we are finding them! This book will show you how."

Dale Hummel
- Senior Pastor of Wooddale Church (Eden Prairie, Minnesota - USA)

"*Jesus In The Secular World* is full of powerful reminders to examine the posture of our hearts in regards to ministry. I pray that this book will encourage countless believers to see the world through the eyes of Jesus and to bring His light into the darkest places."

Matty Mullins
- Lead Vocalist for Memphis May Fire

"The world has become like a small village. We hear news from all over the world instantly. What is done elsewhere in the world, good or bad, affects us all. A movie produced in Hollywood affects somebody's emotions, thought processes, and actions in Hungary or Honduras. *Jesus in the Secular World* opens our eyes to see these trends and the effects of globalization primarily on global youth, how they share almost similar culture, and the needs of the secular world. Writing from a practical point of view and sharing his personal stories of courage and commitment to introduce Jesus in some of the most hostile places of the world, Ben shows all who follow Jesus how to effectively communicate the unchanging message of the Gospel to the changing world."

Dr. Bekele Shanko
- Vice President, CRU/Chairman, Global Alliance for Church Multiplication

"While much of the Church is wringing their hands about the state of millennials and Generation Z, this book powerfully demonstrates how to move from anxiety to action, from criticism to compassion, and from religious words to powerful communication to an entire generation in need and at risk. My young friend Ben is a practitioner, not a prognosticator; he's making a difference all around the world and he speaks the language of today's culture.

This book is well researched, theologically sound, experientially proven, and a roadmap and source of inspiration for those of us who care deeply about the next generation. I highly recommend it."

Chip Ingram
- Author of The Real God & CEO of Living on the Edge

"I can personally vouch for Ben Pierce and his unique and thoughtful insights into the state of millennials and Generation Z. He is not writing theoretically here—he and his entire family are in "the fray" and being used by God to powerfully reach "the most secularized" in our culture. He is a trustworthy guide and should be listened to by anyone struggling to connect with the next generation. Read this book and be INSPIRED and EQUIPPED! Ben is the real deal!"

Troy Dobbs
- Senior Pastor, Grace Church (Eden Prairie, Minnesota - USA)

"There is no band in the world like No Longer Music! With passion & compassion for the dark and unreached spaces of global culture, NLM dares to go and do. Who better to lead this next-gen wave of outreach than the 'son of Steiger' Ben

Pierce! His around-the-world exploits and well-earned insights in advancing the Kingdom will no doubt inspire and fire you up!"

Sy Rogers
- Itinerant Speaker, Former Teaching Pastor of the Multi-Campus LIFE Church & Leadership College (Auckland, New Zealand)

"Ben Pierce reminds us that the youth of today - though most of them live within sight of a church building and have access to the Bible in their own language - are so isolated by secular culture that they are essentially an unreached people group. They deserve and need our attention.

Ben's life follows the example of Jesus, who with vision crossed a lake, faced a storm, encountered a legion, experienced the disfavor of the community... and yet spoke peace, called forth truth, and in God's power, proclaimed liberty. As a result, a man who was otherwise beyond hope met God in His Son, the Lord Jesus, and went on to tell others of His power and authority (Luke 8:22-39).

It is a joy to see Ben so forcefully reaching into secular youth culture through Steiger, and it's a privilege to partner with them in small ways in their work. I commend this book to you and ask you to pray that those who may seem unreachable will indeed meet Jesus and come to sit at His feet."

Blair T. Carlson
- Former International Crusade Director, Billy Graham Evangelistic Association

"If you want to actually understand how to reach the global youth culture today, Ben Pierce is your guy. Not only does he have the experience in actually reaching youth all around the world, but he is also a phenomenal thinker and passionate follower of Christ. Our youth of today need you to read this book!"

David Sorn
- Lead Pastor (Renovation Church, Blaine, MN)

"*Jesus in the Secular World* is an eye-opening revelation about what happens to an entire culture when you remove the objective truth of Jesus and replace it with the idol of individual subjectivism. Ben Pierce shares a testimony that reveals the drastic need for people to be introduced to a Savior. To shatter the misconceptions and abuses created by religion, we must show all people the heart of Jesus, and that is what Ben provides us within this fearless book!"

Ben Utecht
- 2006 Super Bowl Champion, Author, Speaker, and Singer

JESUS IN THE SECULAR WORLD

REACHING A CULTURE IN CRISIS

BEN PIERCE

Cover design: Derek Thornton
Author's photo: Josh Privette
Interior design: Vanessa Mendozzi

Published and distributed by
Steiger International

Tayva, Macklin, and Lenna, this is for you.
My prayer is that this book will produce world-changers
and that you will be among them.

Contents

INTRODUCTION

I spent my teenage years in New Zealand, which is a largely secular country. Despite its incredible natural beauty, it's a dark place filled with domestic violence, alcoholism, and racial tension, and its rate of teen suicide is significantly higher than that of any other country in the developed world.

In my high school, being a Christian was very difficult; in fact, the label was used as a generic insult. I didn't know a single person in my entire class who followed Jesus, and, being desperate to fit in, I didn't exactly advertise the fact that I did. I was happy to get past this time in my life with my faith intact, and I witnessed firsthand the harrowing reality of a post-God environment.

Twelve years after leaving, I had the privilege of going back to New Zealand as the frontman and guitarist for the evangelistic band No Longer Music. This unique group is part of a worldwide missions organization dedicated to reaching and discipling young people outside the church. Our local team had organized a nationwide tour of New Zealand, and I was excited to bring the hope of the gospel to the place where I had grown up.

One of our shows took us right into the middle of the darkness—to a town called Hawera, on the west coast of the North Island. Within just a few months, four teenagers had committed suicide, bringing the community to its knees. A small group of Christians began to pray that God would move in the midst of the devastation. When they heard we were coming to New Zealand, they invited us to join them in their efforts to bring hope to these hurting people.

We played in a warehouse that could have held thousands, so when less than a hundred people showed up, we were a little disappointed. Caleb, our videographer, interviewed one young couple before the show. He asked them why they had come, and they said they were excited to see a rock show but had no interest in God or Christianity.

The small-town crowd seemed stunned by the intensity of our show, and I wasn't sure how they would react to the message. David, who is my dad and the leader of No Longer Music, preached boldly and shared that only the humble will see God. He asked the crowd to stand if they wanted to receive Jesus, and seventeen people stood up! Among those who responded were the young couple Caleb had interviewed prior to the show. We were able to talk with them afterward, and their attitudes had changed completely.

I asked the girl why she had responded, and she said

something inside her had changed and that she felt happy. You could sense a lightness that had not been there at the beginning of the show. They both said this night would completely change their lives.

This experience encapsulates the mission of my life. Yes, the secular world is real and increasingly hostile towards Christianity, but, if we are willing to be bold, God will use us to share his love with the lost.

My experience is not unique. We live in a broken world that is desperate for the truth. There is hope, but in order to make a difference, we need to better understand the people around us.

We Are Losing Them

According to the book *Churchless*, "More than one-third of America's adults are essentially secular in belief and practice."[1] This means there are approximately 156 million Americans who are "not engaged with a church."

A recent study in the United Kingdom showed that 71 percent of people between the ages of eighteen and twenty-four now identify as having no religious beliefs of any kind.[2] According to

---

1   George Barna and David Kinnaman, *Churchless* (Carol Stream, IL: Tyndale Momentum, 2014), 16.

2   Tom Powell, "More than half of Britons 'have no religion', survey reveals," *Evening Standard*, September 4, 2017, https://www.standard.co.uk/news/uk/more-than-half-of-britons-have-no-religion-survey-re-veals-a3626896.html.

Operation World, a growing majority of European countries, including France, the Czech Republic, and Spain,[3] are composed of 1 percent or fewer evangelical Christians.

Much of the formerly "Christian" world is leaving its roots behind and is dominated by secularism (death to religion) and relativism (death to truth). The Bible is no longer considered *the* moral compass; rather, everyone is free to decide for themselves what is right and wrong.

Young people see the church as irrelevant to their day-to-day lives: a dead, empty tradition of the past. As a result, a cultural divide exists between secular youth culture and the church.

As followers of Jesus, it's clear that we need to respond—but how?

We Aren't Finding Them

It's important to understand that with respect to their views of God, non-Christians can range from positive to indifferent to hostile; yet most outreach efforts are focused on reaching those who are already open to the idea of God. Evangelistic events will frequently be held inside a church building and feature the

---

3   Jason Mandryk, "France," Operation World, 2018, http://www.operationworld.org/country/fran/owtext.html ,Jason Mandryk, "Czech Republic," Operation World, 2018, http://www.operationworld.org/country/czec/owtext.html, Jason Mandryk, "Spain," Operation World, 2018, http://www.operationworld.org/country/spai/owtext.html.

latest Christian entertainment in an attempt to attract nonbelievers. This may serve to draw those who are sympathetic or
nominal, but it doesn't reach those who are either apathetic or
anti-God. This is a problem, because it's where our world is
heading—and fast.

Consider the spectrum below. Steiger, the ministry of which
I am part, is dedicated to reaching those at the right end of the
spectrum: those who are growing more distant from the church
every day.

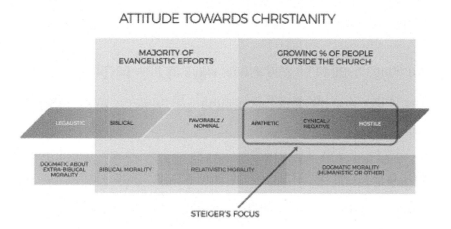

ATTITUDE TOWARDS CHRISTIANITY

The purpose of this book is to highlight the state of secular
culture today and to mobilize more Christians to relevantly reach
those who would not come to the church for answers.

Why Should You Listen to Me?

The material in this book started as a class my brother and I
began teaching a few years ago. The first time we taught our *Jesus*

in the Secular World class, I was reluctant. I had just come back from a five-month tour with No Longer Music. When it came time to teach, I was tired and unprepared, but, by God's grace, it went extremely well. The class was raw and undeveloped, but it was clear that God was with us. Since then, we have taught the class many times, and the timing has felt right to put our thoughts down in writing.

There are many great books written on this subject, so inevitably I wrestled with the question "Do I have anything to add?" Ultimately, I decided I needed to write this book, and there are a couple of reasons why.

Old things need to be said in new ways by new people.

I recently saw a picture of my grandpa holding my mom when she was a little girl. It was incredible. He was an uncanny replica of today's hipster. If *that* version of my grandpa walked into a trendy Minneapolis coffee shop, he would be indistinguishable from the other customers. Truthfully, the hipsters of today copied him, and it reminded me that "there is nothing new under the sun."[4]

This biblical truism encouraged me—even if I tried to contribute something original, I wouldn't. Embracing this was incredibly freeing. Rather than inventing something new, I'm relaying a message about which I'm very passionate. Essentially, I decided to write this book because old truths need to be said

---

4 Eccles. 1:9.

in new ways by new people.

Furthermore, old truths need to be applied to new times for new people. The principles laid out in this book are basic biblical concepts but are written with today's culture and context in mind. This is critical because both the secular world and followers of Jesus are different than they were a hundred years ago. They face unique challenges and have specific strengths and weaknesses. My hope is that my message in this book has been framed in a way that will resonate with the realities of the twenty-first century.

I have seen this played out in my life.

This is not a book of spiritual theories I've thought up; these are principles derived from the life I've lived. I have been in full-time ministry for ten years and have seen God move powerfully in the secular world.

But the origins of this book go back further. My parents are originally from Minnesota, in the United States. They met in Amsterdam while working with Youth With A Mission (a Christian missions organization). Not long afterward, they married and decided to stay in Amsterdam to engage in full-time ministry. That's where my brother and I were born.

My parents felt called to reach the unreached underground culture in Amsterdam. The dominant social movement of the time was that of the punks and anarchists. These young people rallied around social rebellion and fighting against "the system."

Not unlike the secular youth culture of today, they had a very negative view of God and the church.

My mom and dad devoted sixteen years to reaching these young people for Jesus, and, thankfully, they didn't shelter us from their life's work. My brother and I experienced faith in action on a daily basis. Our parents demonstrated what an authentic relationship with God looks like. They modeled radical obedience to Jesus, and we witnessed the transforming power of God at work in real time. We were not bystanders to my parents as they did ministry. It was the family business, and everyone was expected to contribute.

I remember going on tour with No Longer Music as a young kid and seeing people giving their lives to Jesus every night. I recall how seriously I took my job of handing my dad his microphone before the show. I wrote my first song for the show at age fifteen. I was probably really annoying to the other band members, but my parents didn't care. They were determined to show my brother and me that following Jesus was exciting, dynamic, risk-filled, and anything but a dead tradition of the past.

Since then, I have seen people kneeling in the main square of Reykjavík, Iceland; praying to receive Jesus in Beirut, Lebanon; and responding to the gospel in cities from Moscow to Madrid to Warsaw. I have prayed with tattooed, hardcore guys in São Paulo, Brazil, gang members in New Zealand, and thousands of "ordinary" young people all over the world.

I have literally lived and breathed radical ministry my whole life, and this immense privilege has given me a perspective that I believe is worth sharing.

What Should You Expect from This Book?

Let me start with what you should not expect.

This book is not an academic thesis or an in-depth study on secularism; that has been covered extensively by more qualified writers.

It also is not a formulaic "Five-Step Program for Reaching Non-Christians." Ten years of ministry, as well as a lifetime of seeing it in action, has made it abundantly clear to me that reaching people is not about having the correct methodology.

There simply isn't a one-size-fits-all approach for reaching the secular world. I hope to give you the "gas," not the "car." What fuels all of us will be the same, but how that translates into each particular context will be different.

One of my favorite narratives in the Old Testament is the life of Nehemiah. His example provides a blueprint for how godly men and women should respond to dire circumstances. It's worth breaking down.

Nehemiah 1:1 establishes the plot. The Jewish people were in exile, Jerusalem was in ruins, and the city wall had been destroyed. Nehemiah's brother shared this desperate situation with him, and his response is striking:

"As soon as I heard these words I sat down and wept and mourned for days, and I continued fasting and praying before the God of heaven."[5]

Jerusalem was in a bad state, and a solution was needed urgently, but, rather than rushing to act, Nehemiah "sat down and wept and mourned for days" and then continued to pray. Some historians estimate that Nehemiah may have prayed for several months before acting.[6] He understood that if his attempts to solve the problem were not fueled by God's power and motivated by his love, they would accomplish nothing. Once Nehemiah had God's heart, he made a plan and set out to make a difference.

This book aims to follow the model his life set out.

If there is anything I hope people get from this book, it's this: the spiritual needs of the world are overwhelming, and God wants to use everybody to make a difference. The church *knows* far more than it *does*. I believe it's time we heed James and become "doers of the word" not just "hearers."[7] I sense a growing dissatisfaction among believers who are tired of a weak faith that has no impact on the world.

There is hunger in the church to make a difference, but

---

5   Neh. 1:4.

6   Scholars have estimated that the period of "some days" is probably four months. In 1:1, he says, "In the month of Chislev in the twentieth year . . ." In 2:1, when he begins to take action, he refers to the month of Nisan, four months later.

7   James 1:22.

Christians still struggle to step out and do something. I believe this is because while many Christians get the *why*, they struggle with the *how*. My prayer is that this book will awaken the indifferent and equip the eager to transform a lost world for Jesus.

2 Chronicles 16:9 says, "For the eyes of the Lord range throughout the earth to strengthen those whose hearts are fully committed to him" (NIV).

Consider the power of those words. The omnipotent Creator of the universe is actively looking for men and women who will give him their whole hearts so he can strengthen them as they step out. My hope is that this book will help draw your heart closer to God, so you can experience his amazing power as you take risks to reach the secular world for Jesus.

It starts by remembering that we serve a powerful God who is not impressed with global trends or great odds. The church has everything it needs to spark a massive spiritual awakening. The solution, however, is not another method or creative approach, but rather men and women falling on their knees, crying out to God, and responding in obedience to his plan.

Who Is This For? Everyone!

A few years back, after I had just finished teaching the *Jesus in the Secular World* class, a woman came up to me and asked for a few minutes of my time. She had attended the full five-week course with her husband, and she explained that, while they had both enjoyed it, they'd initially struggled with how they should respond.

"At first, I distanced myself from your illustrations," she said. "I was inspired by them but didn't see how they applied to my life. But then my husband and I began to pray and ask God what it would look like for us to be reaching those around us. Soon enough, the answer was obvious."

She told me that they managed a McDonald's, and that, as they prayed, God opened their eyes to their employees, many of whom were hurting and broken, and all of whom desperately needed the love of Jesus. They realized that making a difference meant having the courage to reach those right in front of them.

She thanked me and said they were both excited to see how God would move through them in the days ahead.

Talking to this woman reminded me that the principles in this book are not only for unique people with extraordinary callings—they're for everyone. I sincerely believe that the contents of this book will equip you to transform the particular context in which God has put you.

The needs of the world are too many for some followers of Jesus to be merely spectators. God calls all of us to be used by him to make a difference.

1
UNDERSTANDING THE NEED

I remember thinking, "Rock and roll in Iraq? How is that going to work?" None of us really knew what to expect, but the door had opened for us to go. My time with the evangelistic band No Longer Music had introduced me to some unusual places (my first tour was in Kyrgyzstan), but Iraq would be taking things to a whole new level.

We landed in Erbil, a major city in northern Iraq, and it was hot and dusty—this I had expected. What was strange was how "normal" everything else seemed. We were in the Middle East, but the shows could just as well have been in Berlin. Kids wearing jeans and band T-shirts lined the stage, and they videoed or took photos of every moment on their phones, to later post on Facebook. Most of our crowd had only ever seen a live rock band on YouTube, and you could tell how grateful they were that we had come. More importantly, these young people were open to the gospel, and during our tour many prayed to receive Jesus!

This experience was eye-opening. For me, the "globalized youth culture" (a term frequently used by our organization) might have been an interesting theory until that point, but at that show, it became an evident fact. If youth were the same in Iraq as they were in Minneapolis, then the debate as to whether a globalized youth culture existed was settled.

In ten years of using art and music to share the gospel outside the church, I have become convinced of two things:

1. *There has never been a more unified youth culture than there is today.*
2. *Secular young people, if given the chance, WILL respond to the gospel.*

If we are going to reach people, we need to know them. That is the purpose of this first chapter—getting to know the secular world and the youth that populate it.

The pages that follow will serve as an overview of the trends and characteristics that define the secular world today. Needless to say, this is only a broad-stroke summary of an entire culture, but hopefully it will provoke and inspire those of us in the church to get outside its walls and learn how to share Jesus in a relevant way.

The Three Philosophical Pillars

We live in a time of unprecedented connectedness. Mainstream media, global economic strategies, and, above all, the Internet have eroded cultural boundaries. Young people are more similar than ever. At the heart of any culture are the core ideas that form its view of the world. For the globalized youth, these core ideas are secularism, relativism, and tolerance.

Secularism

It's important to understand that secularism is not the total absence of God. Secularism is more accurately characterized by the marginalization and privatization of spirituality.[8] Young people aren't consciously rejecting God per se—they just don't think about God.

Appropriately, religious researchers have dubbed these post-God young people "the nones"—a generation without any religious affiliations.

Religion and Christianity are irrelevant to their day-to-day lives. At best, they see Jesus as a good person or teacher, and at worst, as a symbol of repression and bigotry. "Just over 60 percent of millennials say that Christianity is 'judgmental,' and 64 percent say that 'anti-gay' best describes most churches today."[9]

False perceptions of God leading to the mass secularization of young people is perhaps the greatest challenge to the church today. Not only has religion been relegated to the sidelines of societal relevance, but it also has become something strictly private.

David Wells says, "It's axiomatic that secularism stops the

---

8   D. A. Carson, *The Gagging of God* (Grand Rapids, MI: Zondervan, 1996), 37.

9   Dr. Alex McFarland, "Ten reasons millennials are backing away from God and Christianity," *Fox News*, April 30, 2017, http://www.foxnews.com/opinion/2017/04/30/ten-reasons-millennials-are-backing-away-from-god-and-christianity.html.

life of the divine, but it is important to see that it does so by relocating the divine in the part of the life which is private."[10]

It's not that secular culture hasn't kept some of its spirituality—it just isn't discussed. The more ambiguous a person's faith, the better, and in a culture where supposedly everything goes, specific spiritual convictions do not. It's not that God has vanished; he's just lost his seat at the table.

Relativism

The second defining worldview of secular culture is relativism. Relativism is the idea that there is no transcendent truth and therefore no universal morality. Concepts such as right and wrong and justice and duty are social constructs and ultimately illusory. With traditional ethics swept aside, relativism is an absolute pillar of the globalized youth culture. "You have your opinion and I have mine" is the slogan of our day. It doesn't have to make sense; just don't violate it.

Ironically, the only truth that is not relative is that truth is relative. Secular people have no problem embracing two mutually exclusive perspectives, as long as doing so serves the way they want to live. It's the ultimate "have your cake and eat it, too" philosophy. Relativism has become a dominant force entrenched in the minds of young people.

---

10   David F. Wells, *No Place for Truth* (Grand Rapids, MI: Inter-Varsity, 1993), 79.

Allan Bloom, in *The Closing of the American Mind*, points out the following: "There is one thing a professor can be absolutely certain of: almost every student entering the university believes, or says he believes, that truth is relative. If this belief is put to the test, one can count on the students' reaction—they will be uncomprehending. That anyone should regard the proposition as not self-evident astonishes them, as though he were calling into question 2+2=4."[11]

If followed to its logical end, moral relativism would lead to unmitigated evil and a total collapse of society, and yet this hasn't happened. This is because no one lives as if relativism were true. Notions of right and wrong and justice and duty are familiar themes in entertainment and pop culture, speaking to the larger rejection of relativism as a practical way to live.

Even secular writers seem to agree. Consider the thoughts of Helen Rittelmeyer, writer for the *American Spectator*, who says, "Overprocessed chart-slayers like Katy Perry and Ke$ha don't act as if they want to be judged by the brutal honesty of their self-expression, and neither do mannered indie darlings like the Decemberists. As for cinema, anti-heroes are out and heroes are back in. Virtue, authority, and law and order are all in fashion, as the bank accounts of Chris Nolan, J.K. Rowling, and Marvel

---

11   Allan Bloom, *The Closing of the American Mind* (New York, NY: Simon and Schuster, 1987), 19.

Comics will attest."[12]

It is almost impossible to find someone truly committed to moral relativism in Hollywood or elsewhere. What you find in abundance, however, are people who say that morals are relative and yet live as though they are not. Secular young people haven't abandoned morals and duties; rather, they have rejected traditional moral anchors and reference points, creating a value system of their own.

Jonathan Merritt argues in the *Atlantic* that "instead of being centered on gender roles, family values, respect for institutions and religious piety, [the modern notion of morality] orbits around values like tolerance and inclusion. (This new code has created a paradoxical moment in which all is tolerated except the intolerant and all included except the exclusive.)"[13]

Relativism is an important, unifying characteristic of secular young people in theory, not in practice. Though it hasn't produced the moral monsters and philosophical nihilists that it should have, it has given rise to another foundational belief of secular young people: tolerance.

---

12   Helen Rittelmeyer, "Moral Relativism, R.I.P.," *American Spectator*, September 17, 2012, https://spectator.org/35020_moral-relativism-rip/.

13   Jonathan Merritt, "The Death of Moral Relativism," *Atlantic*, March 25, 2016, http://www.theatlantic.com/politics/archive/2016/03/the-death-of-moral-relativism/475221/.

Tolerance

We are told to be open-minded, and this sounds noble on the surface. Every idea, belief, and view is equal and should be respected by all people everywhere. It doesn't take a professional philosopher to see the self-refuting nature of this ideology. Tolerance is the logical extension of relativism, and it shares its incoherence. After all, demanding the tolerance of all views isn't very tolerant.

As D. A. Carson points out, "[Open-mindedness] no longer means that you may or may not have strong views yet remain committed to listening honestly to countervailing arguments. Rather, it means you are dogmatically committed to the view that all convictions that any view whatsoever is wrong are improper and narrow-minded."[14]

The best form of tolerance is an ability or willingness to listen to people with beliefs and opinions that differ from your own. In the past, people were sacred, while ideas were up for debate. Today, tolerance guards ideas and attacks people. This has created a climate of conformity. People no longer have the freedom to think critically about issues and come to their own conclusions, for fear of being rejected or bullied. Tolerance suddenly isn't so tolerant.

In a culture dominated by secularism, relativism, and tolerance

---

14   Carson, *The Gagging of God*, 35.

(at least as it is liberally defined and applied), it is no wonder that Christianity, with its exclusive truth claims and absolutes, is incompatible. More and more young people reject Christianity because to follow Jesus is to swim against the current of our times—the road is too narrow, the cost too high.

Culture's emancipation from God hasn't come without a cost. When God "died," he didn't die alone. Without something transcendent to define truth and in which to ground right and wrong, secular morality has decayed at astounding speeds. The loss of God came with a loss of identity. Value and purpose, previously found in God, are now up for grabs, and young people have been discovering that freedom from God hasn't necessarily made them free.

Even as the New Atheists parade their emancipation from God, they forget that those who paved the path to secularism did so with a profound understanding of the devastating consequences. Consider the haunting sentences that follow Nietzsche's famous proclamation.

"God is dead. God remains dead. And we have killed him. How shall we comfort ourselves, the murderers of all murderers? What was holiest and mightiest of all that the world has yet owned has bled to death under our knives: who will wipe this blood off us? What water is there for us to clean ourselves? What festivals of atonement, what sacred games shall we have to invent? Is not the greatness of this deed too great for us? Must we ourselves not become gods simply to appear worthy of it?"[15]

The irony is that in killing one God we created millions more, and it turns out we make pretty lousy gods.

How Did We Get Here?

The views that define modern youth culture can largely be traced back to the Enlightenment of the eighteenth century. In the absolute monarchies of Europe, life had a very fixed order. God was at the center, then came the ruling elite, and then everyone else. They believed that God himself ordained this hierarchy and (rather conveniently) legitimized the authority of the aristocracy. To question it was to question God, and so for hundreds of years this system remained mostly unchallenged.

The Enlightenment turned the whole system on its head (removing a lot of heads, as well!) and instead put man at the center. This was the birth of humanism. While many atrocities were committed in its name, it also generated many positive advances for equality. Issues such as workers' rights, for example, became front and center, and authority was no longer beyond challenge. Many of America's founding ideals are owed to the French Enlightenment movement.

This caused a seismic shift in the Western world. While for most, God initially still remained at the center, with each passing

---

15   Friedrich Nietzsche, *The Gay Science*, ed. Walter Kaufmann (New York: Vintage, 1974),181–82.

day man became more the focus. America's founding documents capture the Enlightenment's dual ideology of God's supreme deity and of man's elevated status.

"We hold these truths to be self-evident, that all men are created equal, that they are endowed by their Creator with certain unalienable Rights, that among these are Life, Liberty and the pursuit of Happiness."[16]

A key feature of this thinking was that man's value and rights do not dethrone God, but are in fact grounded in him. Far from validating the abuse of power, God endows each person with unique value and protects these rights from injustice imposed by human rulers.

Enlightenment thinkers and philosophers continued to push the envelope, and it wasn't long before the very authority of God came into question. After all, removing celestial powers is the logical next step after deposing earthly ones. I believe, however, that the motives behind this were not logical, but moral.

Take God out of the picture, and now we are free to do anything we want—no more cosmic judge to infringe on our lives. Many famous secular humanists expressed the joy of their newfound freedom. Consider this candid admission by English philosopher Aldous Huxley: "I had motives for not wanting the world to have meaning; consequently assumed it had none, and

---

16   The United States Declaration of Independence, 1776.

was able without any difficulty to find satisfying reasons for this assumption. For myself, as no doubt for most of my contemporaries, the philosophy of meaninglessness was essentially an instrument of liberation . . . We objected to the morality because it interfered with our sexual freedom."[17]

The emancipation from God himself was the final philosophical leap to full-blown secular humanism—from God at the center, to man and God at the center, to just man and no God.

The globalized youth culture has grown up in the wake of this spiritual revolution, and it has had an enormous impact on who they are and on how they live.

So What Are They Actually Like?

The core beliefs of secular young people produce a shared sense of identity, and they affect their attitudes and behaviors in destructive ways. To reach this culture with the gospel, we must understand it.

Those in the globalized youth culture are between the ages of seventeen and thirty-five and can be found in every major city. They represent more than one billion people, and, despite being spread out all over the world, they are more connected than ever. They generally dress the same, watch the same movies, and listen to the same music, and, as a result, they look and act alike.

---

17   Aldous Huxley, *Ends and Means* (New York, NY: Harper Brothers Publishers, 1937), 273.

They Are Connected

The greatest global connector of them all is the Internet. It is bringing people "together" unlike at any other time in history. We are able to access media and information as never before, and the globalized youth culture is taking full advantage. According to a 2017 eMarketer report, Americans are now spending "12 hours and 7 minutes a day consuming media."[18]

A study done in the United Kingdom in 2015 showed that those aged between sixteen and twenty-four are spending an average of twenty-seven hours online per week, which is an increase of seventeen hours from 2005.[19] Another study showed that young Australians spend up to ten hours a day on Internet-connected devices.[20]

This is a worldwide reality

Social media is one of the most popular online activities for young people today. "As of the second quarter of 2018, Facebook

---

18   "US Adults Now Spend 12 Hours 7 Minutes a Day Consuming Media," *eMarketer*, May 1, 2017, https://www.emarketer.com/Article/US-Adults-Now-Spend-12-Hours-7-Minutes-Day-Consuming-Media/1015775.

19   Elizabeth Anderson, "Teenagers spend 27 hours a week online: how internet use has ballooned in the last decade," *Telegraph*, May 11, 2015

20   Broede Carmody, "Australians spend 10 hours a day on internet connected devices: The digital trends your SME needs to know," *Smart Company*, February 4, 2016,

had 2.23 billion monthly active users."[21] The average time spent daily on Facebook by its users is fifty minutes. This may not sound like a huge number, but according to the U.S. Bureau of Labor, that is the second highest amount of time spent on any leisure activity, behind TV (2.8 hours a day in 2017). It drastically exceeds the average time spent reading (10 minutes for young people) or exercising (17 minutes) each day, and it nearly rivals time spent eating and drinking (1.24 hours a day)![22]

The statistics are resoundingly clear: young people are online a lot and consuming an incredible amount of media. If the age-old adage "You are what you eat" is true, then young people today are being shaped by social media and online entertainment, and the impact is far from innocuous. Their online behavior is having a permanent effect on their brains. According to Nicholas Carr in his book *The Shallows*, our brains are not fixed, as they once

---

21   "Number of monthly active Facebook users worldwide as of 2nd quarter 2018 (in millions)," *Statista*, 2018, https://www.statista.com/statistics/264810/number-of-monthly-active-facebook-users-world-wide/.

22   James B. Stewart, "Facebook Has 50 Minutes of Your Time Each Day. It Wants More," *New York Times*, May 5, 2016, https://www.nytimes.com/2016/05/06/business/facebook-bends-the-rules-of-audience-engagement-to-its-advantage.html; United States Department of Labor, "American Time Use Survey Summary," *U.S. Bureau of Labor Statistics*, June 28, 2018, https://www.bls.gov/news.release/atus.nr0.htm; United States Department of Labor, "American Time Use Survey Summary," *U.S. Bureau of Labor Statistics*, June 28, 2018, https://www.bls.gov/news.release/archives/atus_06282018.pdf.

were thought to be, but can in fact be rewired. He writes: "As particular circuits in our brain strengthen through the repetition of a physical or mental activity, they begin to transform that activity into a habit. The paradox of neuroplasticity, observes Dr. Norman Doidge, is that for all the mental flexibility it grants us, it can end up locking us into 'rigid behaviors.'"[23]

Carr believes the negative effects are many. "When we go online, we enter an environment that promotes cursory reading, hurried and distracted thinking, and superficial learning."[24]

I have experienced the rewiring effect of the Internet in my own life. I remember being able to focus on one thing at a time for a long time, but now I am constantly multitasking: Skype calls while driving, texting while watching a movie, writing lyrics while listening to a podcast—one time, I had a conference call while driving a lawn mower. It's out of control. The Internet is negatively affecting our ability to concentrate. Content is delivered in constantly evolving bursts, and every article links to another set of articles, further encouraging the reader to leap from page to page rather than focus in one place for a prolonged period. The Internet has changed our brains, and, now that it has, we keep going back to it because it provides the only kind of content we can handle—it's a vicious cycle. We are experiencing

---

23   Nicholas Carr, *The Shallows* (New York, NY: Norton, 2011), 34.

24   Carr, *The Shallows*, 115.

an epidemic of distraction.

Virtually every facet of our lives receives less concentrated attention than it did two decades ago.[25]

They Are Socially Isolated

The negative impact of the Internet is perhaps most forcefully felt in relationships. MIT author Sherry Turkle wrote a brilliant and exhaustive study on the effects of technology on our relationships. She states, "We build a following and wonder to what degree our followers are friends. We recreate ourselves as online personae and give ourselves new bodies, homes, jobs, and romances. Yet, suddenly, in the half-light of virtual community, we may feel utterly alone."[26]

The sad irony is that the Internet, while connecting the whole world, has left us more isolated than ever. So much so that many young people prefer the distance of virtual relationships to the messiness of the real thing.

"Young people are among the first to grow up with an expectation of continuous connection, and they are among the first to grow up not necessarily thinking of simulation as second best."[27]

---

25   Barna and Kinnaman, *Churchless*, 18.

26   Sherry Turkle, *Alone Together* (New York, NY: Basic Books, 2011), 11.

27   Turkle, *Alone Together*, 17

They Are Obsessed with Fame and Being Followed

Perhaps most tragic is that while young people feel isolated and alone, they believe the lie that everyone "out there" is beautiful, famous, and happy. Online content is tirelessly curated, edited, and filtered. The best moments are captured and shared, and only the most beautiful pictures are posted.

Is it any wonder that when young people compare their lives with the fictional lives displayed on social media, they don't measure up?

Social media has created the illusion that we are all on the edge of stardom. Young people today are obsessed with the fame of others and desire above all else to be "followed." This has bred a culture of narcissism perhaps unlike any other in history, in which the youth culture believes the most mundane parts of their lives are worth sharing. "Social networks instruct us to share whenever there's something on our minds," says Turkle, "no matter how ignorant or ill-considered, and then help us broadcast it to the widest possible audience."[28]

The ancient maxim "I think, therefore I am" should be replaced with "I post, therefore I am." For young people today, capturing a moment and posting it online has existential meaning.

As the psychotherapist Michael Hausauer notes: "Teens and other young adults have a terrific interest in knowing what's

---

28   Turkle, *Alone Together*, 276.

going on in the lives of their peers, coupled with a terrific anxiety about being out of the loop. If they stop sending messages, they risk becoming invisible."[29] The Internet and social media are producing a culture of distracted, self-focused, and socially isolated young people.

They Are Sexually Broken

Young people today are several generations removed from the sexual revolution of the 1960s and 1970s, which jettisoned traditional sexuality and challenged the typical family structure. Sex was no longer expected to take place within the confines of marriage, and the consequences of this shift were devastating. The number of broken families, kids being born out of wedlock, and sexually transmitted diseases soared.[30] Sexual brokenness has always been part of post-fall humanity, but things seem to be worsening at an exponential rate.

There are now no rules.

An entire generation of young people is growing up believing

---

29   Carr, *The Shallows*, 118.

30   "STDs at record high, indicating urgent need for prevention," *Centers For Disease Control and Prevention*, September 26, 2017, https://www.cdc.gov/media/releases/2017/p0926-std-prevention.html; American Psychological Association, "Marriage & Divorce," 2018, http://www.apa.org/topics/divorce/; Joseph Chamie, "Out-of-Wedlock Births Rise Worldwide," *YaleGlobal Online*, March 16th, 2017, https://yaleglobal.yale.edu/content/out-wedlock-births-rise-worldwide.

that sex is meaningless, gender a personal choice, and monogamy a joke. What would have been considered X-rated only a few decades ago is now proudly displayed on storefronts. Violent and sexual content has become so pervasive in mainstream movies that it's nearly impossible to avoid. And then there's pornography—arguably the greatest threat to young people today.

Pornography is a multibillion dollar industry in the US alone. Sixty-four percent of young people between the ages of thirteen and twenty-four actively seek out pornography at least once a week.[31] In the case of boys, the average age of exposure to pornography is between eight and eleven.[32] The globalized youth culture is being raised on explicit sexual images and videos, many of which are violent and all of which degrade and objectify the actors involved.

The findings of a joint study conducted by the University of Indiana and the University of Hawaii led to this conclusion: "On the average, individuals who consume pornography more frequently are more likely to hold attitudes conducive to sexual aggression and engage in actual acts of sexual aggression than individuals who do not consume pornography or who consume

---

31   National Center on Sexual Exploitation, *Pornography & Public Health Research Summary*, nAugust 2, 2017, http://endsexualexploitation.org/wp-content/uploads/NCOSE_Pornography-PublicHealth_ResearchSummary_8-2_17_FINAL-with-logo.pdf.

32   The Novus Project, 2018, http://thenovusproject.org/resource-hub/parents.

pornography less frequently."[33]

The accusations against pornography are coming from inside the industry itself. In a recent interview, Pamela Anderson, a former Playboy playmate, said, that "people need more and more to get aroused. I think it's leaning towards violence against women, rape, child abuse."[34]

Mass consumption of pornography is leaving millions of young people with dysfunctional relationships, violent tendencies, and distorted perceptions of sexuality.

A 2011 study showed that 83 percent of men who consumed "mainstream" porn "expressed greater intent to commit rape, should they be assured they wouldn't get caught."[35] It's no surprise that violent sexual crimes committed by young people have increased dramatically in the era of Internet pornography.

Until recently, the highly popular porn site xHamster allowed users to upload videos depicting nonconsensual sex. It wasn't until the infamous Brock Turner case (the Stanford student

33   Dawn Hawkins, "Pornography: The Missing Piece In The Movement Against Sexual Violence," *Huffington Post,* June 21, 2016, https://www.huffingtonpost.com/entry/pornography-the-missing-piece-in-the-movement-against_us_57696ccfe4b06cb7dd543b4c/c.

34   Heather Saul, "Pamela Anderson suggests porn addiction is leading towards violence against women, rape and child abuse," *Independent,* October 14, 2016, https://www.independent.co.uk/news/people/pamela-anderson-porn-addiction-is-leading-towards-violence-and-rape-a7362266.html.

35   Hawkins, "Pornography,nt.c."

convicted of a rape that was largely linked to his consumption of nonconsensual pornography) that xHamster blocked this material under the "Brock Turner" rule.[36]

The fact that this was implemented only after this case went public is shocking and tragic.

They Are Confused

Christianity provides an excellent framework for understanding reality. As followers of Jesus, we know how we got here and why. We have a moral compass, purpose, and hope beyond death.

Young people growing up in the secularized world have no such luxury, and without a solid foundation for origin, meaning, morality, and destiny, they are left to make it up as they go along. Their view of the world tends to be a disjointed amalgamation of vague spirituality and humanism. This leads to cognitive dissonance.

They are desperate for meaning but insist that they are products of chance. They are angry about injustice but refuse to accept any absolute truth. They borrow Christian concepts of morality, human value, and meaning without acknowledging the God in which these concepts are grounded. The globalized youth live with conflicting perspectives, yet don't

---

36   "Xhamster enacts 'Brock Turner rule' banning rape porn site-wide," *Digital Review*, June 11, 2016, http://digitalreview.co/xhamster-enacts-brock-turner-rule-banning-rape-porn-sitewide/.

even seem to notice.

In the past, societal pillars such as teachers, politicians, and pastors shepherded new generations from adolescence to adulthood. Young people today are suspicious of traditional authority figures. They have instead turned to their peers, to online stars, and to celebrities for guidance—but these role models are equally confused.

They Are Consumers

The globalized youth culture grew up watching the dreams of their parents fail them. They saw their parents work exhausting hours, often at the expense of their families, in order to accumulate more and more—leading to stress, unhappiness, and divorce. As a consequence of growing up with parents who were tethered to their high-pressured jobs, big houses, and mortgages, young people have "rebelled" and created their own brand of consumerism: one focused on experiences, pleasure, and technology. They want to be mobile, spontaneous, and unencumbered by the material things that tied down their parents.

Having seen its effects, it's curious that they would not discard consumerism altogether. This is because the root issue remains the same: the reductionism of the secular perspective and an identity in crisis. Secularism strips life of the transcendent and leaves us trying to satisfy spiritual longings in material ways. But it doesn't work.

This is coupled with corporate advertisement strategies that promote feelings of inadequacy. We are meant to feel as if we never have enough and as if what we're missing is within our reach. This vicious marriage between consumption and identity creates an unending appetite and leaves young people feeling perpetually dissatisfied.

It runs much deeper than simply an excess of things; consuming has become an entire identity. In his book *Humble Apologetics*, John Stackhouse writes, "Consumerism is an outlook, a way of seeing things, a way of responding to the world, which frames everything in terms of consumption by oneself."[37]

This is not a hobby or a lifestyle; it is a religion.

When this consumer mentality is brought into relationships, it wreaks havoc. Young people treat their friends and family as products to consume, and, as with any object, the appeal eventually wears off. Sooner rather than later, the relationship no longer offers the satisfaction it once did and is discarded. Consequently, young people's lives are filled with abandoned, fragmented relationships, and they are often entirely unaware of their selfish approach in dealing with people.

Is It All Bad?

Everywhere you look, the emerging generation is being criticized, and often deservedly so. It's clear that this group of young people

---

37   John G. Stackhouse Jr., *Humble Apologetics* (New York, NY: Oxford University Press, 2002), 55.

has unique weaknesses, but so does every other. Ultimately, each generation is lost and in need of the gospel. So if we are going to reach them, we need to look for common ground instead of simply being critical of their shortcomings.

For instance, young people today are highly cause-focused. They are concerned about social justice, the environment, and equality. This passion for change can be an open door for the gospel.

Even secular culture's commitment to relativism can be an opportunity to share your faith. Although they are unwilling to commit to any one religion as ultimately right, those in the globalized youth culture are willing to discuss spiritual things. The lines have blurred, and while getting any consensus or agreement might be difficult, one is far less likely to encounter entrenched fundamentalism in young people today.

There are also unique technological advantages today that can be utilized for kingdom purposes.

The Internet has made it possible to reach millions of people instantly. Social media is being used to share the gospel in places previously impossible to reach, such as conservative Muslim countries. While the Internet has led to much destruction, it has also opened up great opportunity.

In addition, because young people are influenced primarily by American media and entertainment, they are drawn to and understand similar music, symbols, and imagery. No Longer Music's theatrical depiction of the gospel has been equally effective and relevant in over thirty countries on five continents. Incredibly, the language barrier is a shrinking problem. It is amazing how well English is spoken throughout the Western world. Adding a common language to an increasingly common culture makes the phrase "globalized youth culture" more accurate than ever.

What Can Be Done?

It's easy to be overwhelmed by the magnitude of the problem. If you have never felt this way, you've likely never really understood how bad things are.

The odds are better, however, that this is no surprise to you. In fact, you have probably been aware of this for quite some time. For you, the globalized youth culture is not simply an academic theory, but something that involves your brother, sister, cousin, a close friend, or colleague, and your heart breaks for this person.

The good news is that there is hope. "He who is in you is greater than he who is in the world."[38]

We may feel overwhelmed by how lost this culture seems, but God is not.

God is at work redeeming this globalized youth culture as we speak. There are faithful men and women all over the world who are devoting their lives to relevantly reaching these young people

---

38   1 John 4:4.

for Jesus. God has used my life to share his love with hundreds of thousands of secular young people across the world.

If my life is evidence of anything, it's that God desires to use ordinary people to do extraordinary things. My prayer is that this book will not only help you understand the secular culture, but will also equip you to be used by God to redeem it.

But first, we need to know the source of power—or we will accomplish nothing.

2
THE SOURCE OF POWER

The world is a dark place, but God is at work and we are called to participate in his redemptive plan. He has chosen to use you and me, broken and imperfect, to change the world.

How do I know?

Consider the heroes of the Bible: Paul the murderer, King David the adulterer, Jonah the coward, Noah the drunkard. This is an impressive list of sinful, ill-equipped, ill-prepared people accomplishing God's purposes despite themselves.

Too often, Christians rely on hard work, evident gifts, or great strategies to reach the world. We think this way because we are influenced by a business mentality. If a product is successful, it is replicated, so what used to be rare is now everywhere.

In many contexts, such as business, entertainment, and sports, replicating success makes sense.

But should this be happening in the church?

Often, we aren't looking to *God* for a way to reach people; we are looking at what's "working." If a preacher is popular or a worship band anointed, we think we need to deliver those same sermons or sing those same songs. If a particular ministry has a significant impact, we immediately want to know how we can adopt their method.

Tents Are the Key!

In the early days of their ministry, my parents didn't see great results. They were frustrated and began asking God for answers. They felt that he asked them to stop all they were doing—their programs and strategies—and just pray. That's what they did for almost two years. Prayer stopped being *a part* of what they did, and it became *all* they did. They would go out into the forest outside the city and pray all night. They would ask God to show them his plan, give them his heart, and fill them with his power in order to reach the lost in Amsterdam.

What I have experienced, is that real moves of God are built on prayer, not strategy. In this book, you will not find an emphasis on a method or program, because this mentality has led a lot of well-meaning Christians astray. I have seen evidence of this truth my whole life.

Eventually, God led my parents to start a Bible study on a big red boat behind the central train station in Amsterdam. This Bible study became a gathering place for punks, the disenfranchised, and those who would never set foot in a church. Before they knew it, a movement was born. Around the same time, my dad started No Longer Music. Despite being raw and undeveloped, the band began receiving invitations to play in Amsterdam, throughout Europe, and eventually all over the world. The early days in Amsterdam were the beginning of what has now become a worldwide missions organization called Steiger. Prayer birthed the ministry, and prayer is its core value to this day.

After sixteen years in Amsterdam, my parents moved our family to New Zealand—literally the other side of the world. It was during this time that the power of prayer became personal for me.

Growing up in New Zealand as a follower of Jesus wasn't easy. Being the son of missionaries made fitting in even harder. My parents realized that if my faith was going to survive, I would need help. So my dad started a Bible study. Every Wednesday, my brother and I and some of our friends would meet in our living room.

This Bible study wasn't your typical girl-chasing, laser-tag-playing youth group. Not to say there's anything wrong with that; it just wasn't my experience. My dad is intense. He was back then, and he still is now. Everything he does, he does to the fullest—he can't help himself. Our Bible study took on his personality, and this included how we prayed. We were only teenagers, but we prayed hard.

We would buy a bunch of junk food and energy drinks and set up a tent in the forest and pray all night.

During this time, God started to break our hearts for our friends.

I remember one prayer time very clearly. One of the guys

in our group stopped us and said, "I believe God wants us to have a big tent. He wants us to set it up in the middle of the city and invite all of our friends, and they will come and give their lives to him!" We all agreed and were excited about this idea, and we prayed that God would make it happen. A couple of months later, we bought a big circus tent, and a local company donated all the supplies we needed to build a stage. God gave us favor with the local government, and they allowed us to set up in a field in the middle of the city. Every month for almost two years, we would host "The Great Munter Gathering" (don't ask where the name came from—no one knows).

Our vision was ridiculously ambitious, if you consider that it took over a week to set up and several days to pack down and that we did that every month for two years. I'm surprised we survived, but it was great!

The event would feature music, videos, break dancing, and a clear proclamation of the gospel. Every month, kids were giving their lives to Jesus. It was clear God was behind us. At the event's peak, over five hundred young people were coming, and, for a time, this was having a major impact on the whole area.

During one of our gatherings, a total stranger described how he felt as if a magnet had pulled him into the parking lot while he was driving. He'd had no idea that an event was going on, but he said he'd felt compelled to come inside. My dad was preaching, and he invited those who wanted to know Jesus to come to the stage. This guy came forward and gave his life to Jesus.

Stories like this were not uncommon.

God allowed us to share the gospel with thousands of young people and, for a time, to reach our entire city. Why? Were we uniquely qualified or gifted? Did we have a lot of money? No. God used an ordinary group of high school students because we committed ourselves to seeking him with a desperate heart. This solidified my understanding of the power of prayer.

But here's the thing: every time I share this story in a church, someone will come up to me and say, "You know, I've always said tents were the key! We need to have a tent outreach here." I never know how to respond to that. Part of me wants to yell, "Did you listen to anything I said?" Usually, I remind the person of the purpose of my illustration, which is that the strategy is irrelevant and that God can use anyone or anything.

Prayer Isn't Sport

Why is it that we are drawn to quick fixes or five-step programs and often ignore the underlying principles? Every major move of God in my life has begun with prayer. Sadly, so many ministries and outreach programs are ineffective because prayer isn't taken seriously.

Elisabeth Elliot, a lifelong missionary, speaker, and author, wrote a brilliant article on prayer, and it is worth quoting at length.

"People who ski happen to enjoy skiing; they have time for skiing, can afford to ski, and are good at skiing. I have found

that I often treat prayer as though it were a sport like skiing—
something you do if you like it, something you do in your spare
time, something you do if you can afford the trouble, something
you do if you're good at it. Otherwise, you do without it most
of the time. When you get in a pinch you try it, and then you
call an expert.

"But prayer isn't a sport. It's work. Prayer is work because a
Christian simply can't 'make a living' without it. The apostle
Paul said we 'wrestle' in prayer. In the wrestling of a Christian in
prayer, 'our fight is not against any physical enemy; it is against
organizations and powers that are spiritual. We are up against the
unseen powers that control this dark world, and spiritual agents
from the very headquarters of evil.'[39] Seldom do we consider
the nature of our opponent, and that is to his advantage. When
we do recognize him for what he is, however, we have an inkling
as to why prayer is never easy. It's the weapon that the Unseen
Power dreads most, and if he can get us to treat it as casually as
we treat a pair of skis or a tennis racquet, he can keep his hold."[40]

Too many Christians treat prayer as sport, not as work.

This is because the church has been influenced by the world
and its various forms of prayer. We often think of it as a Christian

---

39   Eph. 6:12 (Phillips).

40   Elisabeth Elliot, "Struggling in Prayer," *The Elisabeth Elliot News-
letter*, January/February 2002, http://www.elisabethelliot.org/newslet-
ters/2002-01-02.pdf.

practice, but prayer is a "global phenomenon."[41]

According to a 2017 study, 28 percent of those who have no religious affiliation admitted to praying at least once in the last three months.[42]

As you would expect, nonreligious prayer is self-serving, superficial, and powerless. It has become synonymous with deep thinking or meditation. Prayer in the non-Christian world is a bumper sticker cliché offered up in times of tragedy or need. Secular prayer is not directed at a particular God or spiritual entity as much as to all gods and spiritual entities.

By detaching prayer from any particular God or moral code, the nonreligious can borrow its cathartic qualities without having any of the behavioral obligations that come with a defined, unambiguous faith.

Many Christians have been influenced by this secular brand of prayer. They have an intellectual understanding that prayer should be a regular and dynamic conversation with God, but when it comes down to it, that's *all* it is: intellectual.

Let's be honest: do we take prayer seriously? For many Christians, prayer times are often programmatic and last

---

41   Timothy Keller, *Prayer: Experiencing Awe and Intimacy with God* (New York, NY: Penguin House, 2014), 35.

42   The Barna Group, "Silent and Solo: How Americans Pray," *Barna*, August 15, 2017, https://www.barna.com/research/silent-solo-americans-pray/.

for only a few minutes. There are always exceptions, but too often prayer becomes a routine or a ritual. We pray before meals and at the beginning of meetings, but where is our desperation?

How Do We Get Back on Track?

Learning how to pray starts with having an accurate view of God.

In the first part of Hebrews 11:6, Paul makes an interesting statement: "Anyone who comes to [God] must believe that he exists" (NIV). For years, I skimmed past these crucial words and focused on the latter half of the verse, which says that God rewards those who pray desperately for him.

This was a big mistake. Paul reminds us in 2 Timothy 3:16–17 that "all Scripture is God-breathed and is useful for teaching, rebuking, correcting and training in righteousness, so that the servant of God may be thoroughly equipped for every good work" (NIV).

So why did Paul make this point? It seems a little rudimentary for an audience that believed in God. He made this statement because many claim to believe he exists, but few do.

Jesus warns us in Matthew 7:22–23 that "on that day many will say to me, 'Lord, Lord, did we not prophesy in your name, and cast out demons in your name, and do many mighty works in your name?' And then I will declare to them, 'I never knew you; depart from me, you workers of lawlessness.'"

Others claim to know God, but in reality they follow a

religion of their own making. They reject the biblical view of God, strip the gospel of any exclusionary doctrine, and create a version of the Christian faith to placate the spirit of our age. This false perception of God is certainly easier to accept, but it's untrue.

When you begin to see God for who he really is, your prayer life will come alive! It will no longer feel like an empty ritual or a meaningless act. You will connect with the Creator of the universe. You will build a deep, intimate relationship with the only real source of wisdom, comfort, guidance, and provision. You will know the real God.

But the work doesn't stop there. Even when saved, we need to guard the integrity of our prayer lives. Our sinfulness impairs our view of God, and this, Paul argues, greatly affects how we pray. True prayer recalibrates our minds with what is real. While life has a way of warping our perspective, prayer brings God back into focus and our will into submission, inspiring us to greater worship and obedience.

The challenge is that often our prayers are fixated on our own needs and desires, abilities or inabilities. We so easily forget that life is not only about the here and now. Our circumstances don't limit God, and he doesn't adhere to our preferred schedule.

Tim Keller writes, "We should not decide how to pray on the experiences and feelings we want. Instead, we should do everything possible to behold our God as He is, and prayer will follow. The more clearly we grasp who God is, the more our prayer is shaped and determined accordingly."[43]

We can begin to see God more clearly by reflecting on his greatness as seen in creation. When is the last time you did that?

In Romans 1:20, Paul makes a powerful argument for the existence of God. He says, "For his invisible attributes, namely, his eternal power and divine nature, have been clearly perceived, ever since the creation of the world, in the things that have been made."

I lived in New Zealand for nine years, and it is arguably the most beautiful country in the world. Every time I have the privilege of going back, I am further convinced of Paul's assertion that God is "clearly perceived" in its spectacular natural beauty.

We live in a universe of extraordinary complexity, and yet God simply exhaled and all of it came instantly into existence. Colossians 1:17 says, "In [God] all things hold together." God is more powerful and more creative than we can fathom, and his existence is evident in the smallest of details.

Many prominent scientists have had their atheism shaken upon discovering the precise properties necessary for life to exist and how unlikely it is that this could have happened randomly.

The astrophysicist and atheist Sir Fred Hoyle wrote: "A common sense interpretation of the facts suggests that a super intellect has monkeyed with physics, as well as with chemistry

---

43   Keller, *Prayer*, 62.

and biology, and that there are no blind forces worth speaking about in nature. The numbers one calculates from the facts seem to me so overwhelming as to put this conclusion almost beyond question."[44]

Life is extraordinarily complex, so believing it's a result of a blind process requires tremendous faith. Consider the human eye. As Grant Jeffrey describes in his book *Creation*, "When a baby is conceived in its mother's womb . . . a million microscopic optic nerves begin growing from the eye through the flesh towards the optical section of the baby's brain. Simultaneously, a million optic nerves with a protective sheath similar to fiber-optic cable begin growing through the flesh towards the baby's eye. Each of these one million optic nerves must find and match up to its precise mate to enable vision to function perfectly."[45]

I am amazed by this extraordinary example of precision and fine-tuning and am humbled when I compare that to my attempts to create something. As a musician, I have to write many songs. This process from start to finish is lengthy and difficult. It takes hundreds of hours of trial and error, collaboration, refining, and editing, and when the song is complete, it's decent. Yet God, in an instant, without effort, created everything.

---

44   Fred Hoyle, "The Universe: Past and Present Reflections," *Engineering & Science*, November 1981, 8–12.

45   Grant R. Jeffrey, *Creation* (Colorado Springs, CO: WaterBrook Press, 2003), 40.

Do you believe in this God?

Sometimes I'll be on tour in a city that I've never visited before, and as we ride past people on the street, I will start to feel overwhelmed. There are over seven billion people alive today, and there is so much brokenness—what can I possibly do to make a difference? There are times when I struggle to care for the needs of my own family. I don't have what it takes to fix the world's problems. As I stare out of the window, the whole situation feels hopeless.

And yet God knows all of these people by name—he created each one. He is not overwhelmed by their problems or bothered by their requests. Not only does he hear all those who cry out to him, he also has the power to respond.

Do you believe in this God?

God is beyond any human words used to describe him. He is not the best version of us; he is wholly outside our categories of description. God does not do good things; he is the very essence of goodness. God is not only loving; he also gives love its definition. He cannot learn anything, for he knows everything that can be known. He cannot change—he always was and always will be.

Do you believe in this God?

If God is who the Bible describes him to be—incomprehensible, wise with no equal, everywhere, and with unlimited resources—should this not change how we pray? Moreover, God is both powerful and good. He didn't have to be, but he is. And he is kind and merciful.

The substance of our prayers is inextricably linked to our view of God. If we believe he is indifferent, absent, and incapable, why would we pray? We may use prayer as a last-ditch effort, but we will fail to see it as the powerful spiritual weapon that it is. Without a proper understanding of the God to whom we are praying, our prayers can become misdirected, shallow, and even harmful.

J. B. Phillips puts it this way: "Unless the conception of God is something higher than a magnification of our good qualities, our service and worship will be no more and no less than the service and worship of ourselves."[46]

Having an accurate view of God changes everything.

In his book *The Knowledge of the Holy*, A. W. Tozer writes, "Were we able to extract from any man a complete answer to the question, 'What comes to your mind when you think about God,' we might predict with certainty the spiritual future of that man."[47]

What you think of when you think about God is the most important thing about you. If you see God for who he is, you won't be hindered by obstacles and barriers. You won't get caught

---

46   J. B. Phillips, *Your God Is Too Small* (New York, NY: Touchstone, 1952), 54.

47   A. W. Tozer, *The Knowledge of the Holy* (New York, NY: Harper Collins, 19610), 4.

up in what you have or do not have. It won't be about your talents, your resources, or your circumstances. It is incredibly liberating when you understand that it's about God and his power. When you see God clearly, your prayers will no longer be last-minute or reasonable.

And it gets better. If we could begin to grasp just how amazing God is, and then consider Hebrews 11:6, which says that *this* God, this mind-boggling God *will* reward you if you seek him with a desperate heart, would that not revolutionize our prayer lives?

So what does it mean to seek God with a desperate heart?

Jesus shows us in Luke 11:5–9.

In this powerful parable, you're supposed to imagine yourself as a person needing bread. This seems reasonable enough, except you need this bread at midnight.

Since there was no electricity in first-century Israel, you went to bed as soon as it was dark. Midnight would have been more like what we consider three in the morning, but the point I think Jesus was trying to make is that this was the *least convenient time possible.*

You're not just asking for bread—you're asking for it at a terrible time. Nevertheless, you approach a house and knock on the door. Your panic-stricken neighbor rushes to respond, assuming the worst. After all, who would bother someone at a time like this if it weren't an emergency?

The door swings open, and, before the puzzled look on your neighbor's face subsides, you start to speak. You explain that a friend has stopped by, and you have nothing to give him. You ask the neighbor for bread, but he won't give you any. But you're a punk and won't take no for an answer. "Give me bread!" you persist.

Jesus explains that the neighbor eventually gives in to the person's demands, not because of their friendship, which likely ended shortly after this exchange, but because of his "shameless audacity" or, by my translation, because of the friend's "ridiculous boldness."

There are two key aspects of the friend's request that I think are critical to understanding what desperate prayer looks like.

First, it is unreasonable. God knows and cares about every aspect of your life. He wants the weather to be good for your wedding. He wants your car to start, for you to be able to pay your rent, and for you to get over your cold. These are reasonable requests, and God wants to hear them.

But what Jesus illustrated in Luke 11 is that God wants to hear some *unreasonable* requests—prayers that only he can answer. Prayers that aren't humanly possible.

I believe our prayer requests have become far too reasonable. God wants us to pray some "bread at midnight" prayers.

A few years back, I was in Germany on tour with No Longer Music. Our next stop was to be in Croatia, but the whole tour fell apart a few weeks before we were supposed to go there. I felt frustrated. We had come a long way, transported tons of equipment, and had nothing to do. I remember praying an unreasonable prayer: "God, you know why we're here. We're not trying to make money or be famous. Don't let the enemy win. Open another door!"

Our tours are very complicated to organize. We typically play in the center squares of major European and Middle Eastern cities. Getting permission to use these types of venues can take months. Beyond that, housing and feeding a large crew like ours is not easy and takes a lot of advance planning.

To organize another tour while on the road and in only a week's time made no sense, but this was our unreasonable request. It felt a little like asking for bread at midnight.

As we prayed, God brought to mind an Albanian pastor with whom we had previously worked—a radical man of faith, deeply committed to seeing his country reached for Jesus. We called Sabri and pitched our plan. The conversation went something like this:

"Sabri, I know this is crazy, but we want to come to Albania. Would you be able to organize a tour for us?"

"Yes, when?"

"Next week!"

"OK, I am on vacation in Italy, but I will go home now."

And so God answered our prayers.

We packed up our gear, crammed into four vehicles, and drove over a thousand miles to Albania. With only one week to plan, and no promotion at all, we ended up playing twelve shows in ten days. We performed for over thirteen thousand Albanians, and hundreds of them prayed to receive Jesus.

After one concert, I went out into the crowd with our Australian videographers to interview those who had responded to the gospel. I approached two young guys I had seen pray to receive Jesus. I asked them why they had responded. They explained that they were from Muslim families, but they felt a "power" in our message. One guy said that as he watched our performance, he understood that he was "dirty" and that Jesus could make him clean. This was incredible! I have never heard a non-Christian, let alone a Muslim, so clearly articulate the essence of the gospel.

This tour produced countless stories of life transformation. When we drove away, it was hard to believe that it hadn't even been on our schedule!

Our time in Albania was a vivid reminder of the power of prayer. The tour should never have happened. We should not have been able to tour anywhere with only one week to prepare. Beyond that, young Muslims should not have been open to a clear gospel message presented by a Western rock band during Ramadan (which is the Muslim holy month). None of this made sense. None of this was reasonable. But we do not serve a reasonable God! We serve a God who is not impeded by circumstances. We serve a God who loves to answer prayers that don't make sense.

God wants us to pray unreasonable prayers, because when they're answered, he gets the glory. Our lives should be characterized by fruit that we could never have produced on our own.

Our goal should be for people to say: "I know her. There's no way she could do that."

Earnest prayer is also persistent. Going back to the parable in Luke 11, it's worth noting that the person doesn't give up. Remember, at first the neighbor rejected his request, explaining, "No! My family and I are in bed. I can't give you bread!"

But this person illustrates something crucial about prayer: we should never give up.

Maybe, at one time, you prayed unreasonable prayers. You were young and full of faith and believed God could do big things. You would pray, "God, I want to reach a million people with the message of the cross. God, I want everyone in my family to give their lives to you. God, I want to see you use me to change a whole nation."

But now you know how life works, and you've become more realistic—and you don't pray that way anymore.

God doesn't want you to become reasonable. You don't serve a realistic God; you serve one who holds the universe together with his power. He uses ordinary people to reach entire countries, and he can soften the heart of the most hardened, lost member of your family.

Maybe you still believe that God does the impossible, but you've grown tired of asking. God would say to you, "Don't give up!"

You need to be like the widow before the unjust judge, who "neither feared God nor cared what people thought." Day after day, she stood before him and cried, "Give me justice!" Eventually, the widow wore down the judge with her persistence, and he granted her request.[48]

This is how you should pray, and there's good news: God is nothing like this judge. He eagerly awaits our requests.

Sadly, many of us don't view God this way. We can't possibly imagine that he cares, let alone eagerly waits to hear from us. He must have more important things to do than hear our prayers. The very opposite is true. Psalm 116:1–2 says: "I love the Lord, because he hears my voice and my prayer for mercy. *Because he bends down to listen*, I will pray as long as I have breath!" (NLT; emphasis added).

This verse is incredible. God, who created the heavens and the earth, bends down to hear our prayers! Elsewhere, it says he inclines his ear to us when we pray.

Prayer ultimately reorients our hearts to who God is and who we are. This proper perspective is incredibly liberating. No longer is the responsibility on our shoulders. No longer is our broken world beyond repair. When God breaks our hearts for the needs of his children, we can take courage, because we do not serve an indifferent father.

---

48   Luke 18:1–8.

We serve a God who cries over injustice, and he invites us to partner with him to bring about change. This partnership is not centered on programs, strategies, or methods, but on prayer. Eventually, we do have to do something, but if it doesn't start with seeking God, it will not succeed.

As Edward Bounds succinctly reminds us, "No learning can make up for the failure to pray. No earnestness, no diligence, no study, no gifts will supply its lack. Talking to men for God is a great thing, but talking to God for men is greater still."[49]

Paul reminds us in Ephesians 3:20 that we serve a God who is capable of infinitely more than we could ever ask or hope for.

Nehemiah, when confronted with the plight of his people, fell to his knees and prayed: "O Lord God of heaven, the great and awesome God who keeps covenant and steadfast love with those who love him and keep his commandments, let your ear be attentive and your eyes open, to hear the prayer of your servant that I now pray before you day and night for the people of Israel your servants, confessing the sins of the people of Israel, which we have sinned against you. Even I and my father's house have sinned."[50]

His response to a crisis was to first remind himself of God's faithfulness, as well as man's depravity and need for forgiveness.

---

49   Edward Bounds, *Power Through Prayer* (Chicago, IL: Moody Publishers, 2009), 10.

50   Neh. 1:5–6.

In light of his realigned perspective, he then was able to properly respond. Nehemiah's life illustrates the purpose and power of prayer and how God can use someone who seeks him with a desperate heart.

So How Should I Respond?

As is the case with so many things in life, what is simple is not always easy. If God has convicted you, and you feel as if your prayer life isn't where it needs to be, it's not too late!

I've listed a few thoughts below that I hope will encourage you to get back on track. These aren't rules, per se—just things I've learned from personal experience.

1) You are unique; your prayer life will be, too.

I used to drive my teachers crazy for two main reasons: I could never sit still, and I could never be quiet. This isn't a shock to anyone who knows me. As an adult, I've learned to harness this energy, and fortunately I have a job that requires both qualities. This is how God wired me, and understanding this was critical for me in learning how to pray.

One summer when I was in my early twenties, my dad and I started a new routine. Every day, we would go on long walks and seek God. It was never a program or ritual. Our prayers flowed naturally as we talked about what was going on in our lives.

It was as though we were on a walk with God.

This helped me realize two things about how I'm "wired" to

pray. I need to walk outside and to talk out loud. I'm not the "sit down and pray quietly" type—it just doesn't work for me. My mind wanders, and I become restless and distracted.

After college, I relocated often, but my new prayer discipline stuck with me. When I moved to a new place, I would find a park or a path where I could walk and pray.

The point is, I found a way to seek God that fits with who I am. We are all unique. You have been created by God in a certain way, with a distinct personality. Given this, I'm surprised how often we look to a method or program for how to pray rather than simply saying to God, "I want to seek you; show me the best way to do this."

It is important that you find out how you best connect with God. It doesn't have to look like it does for anybody else. You may need to be alone, or you may need to be surrounded by people. You may need to speak out loud, or to sit quietly. Maybe first thing in the morning is the only time you can be focused, or maybe you're a late-night-prayer kind of person—it doesn't matter. What's important is that you figure out how God has wired you and how you can best connect with him.

2) It takes some learning.

The idea that we need to *learn* how to pray can seem strange at first. After all, shouldn't seeking God just be effortless and organic? In my experience, it hasn't been. I have come to realize that the Holy Spirit will teach you to pray as you devote yourself to this discipline.

In Luke 11, the disciples ask Jesus to teach them how to pray. He didn't rebuke them and say, "What's wrong with you? Praying should be natural and easy!" Instead, he gave them a simple model to follow and demonstrated that prayer takes practice.

To avoid confusion, let me define what I mean by "learning." It has nothing to do with style; it goes much deeper than that. Have you ever been around someone whose prayers seem wordy and inauthentic, as if this person is praying for the benefit of those in the room and not to God? Jesus warns against prayers that are more about impressing those around you than about talking to God.

Learning how to pray has far more to do with your heart than with your words. Jesus makes this clear in Luke 6:45: "The good person out of the good treasure of his heart produces good, and the evil person out of his evil treasure produces evil, for out of the abundance of the heart his mouth speaks."

It's an inside-out process. To change the content of our prayers, we need God to change our hearts, and as with any learning, it's not simply a one-time revelation but a gradual process.

In my own life, I found that as I began to meditate on who God is, my prayers became more about thanking him and less about asking him for things. I would pray for an hour yet find myself "running out of time" to ask God for anything. So, for a season, I just stopped asking. To be clear, bringing our requests before God is a necessary and healthy part of prayer, but for a short time in my life, it just didn't seem as important as simply thanking him.

Learning how to pray has been a long process that continues today, and ultimately the credit for any change belongs to God.

Another key is understanding God's will.

I used to struggle with 1 John 5:14–15, which says: "And this is the confidence that we have toward him, that if we ask anything according to his will he hears us. And if we know that he hears us in whatever we ask, we know that we have the requests that we have asked of him."

The first time I read this, it seemed like an odd principle. If I just ask God for something he already wants, he will give it to me? I had to find out whether this was an extraordinary promise or a semantic trick. It all came down to two key questions: "What is God's will for me?" and "Does he have my best interests in mind?"

The answers became clearer as I grew in my faith and my understanding of Scripture. I started to pray 1 John 5 with confidence, knowing that his will for me is good and that I could trust him.

As I learned more of God's promises, I would pray them back to him, knowing that he not only hears me, but will answer. I'd pray: "God, I don't want to be in bondage to sin. Help me to be obedient"—knowing he would. I'd pray: "God make me a better husband. Make me less selfish and use my life to reach the secular world for Jesus"—knowing without a doubt that he heard me and would answer my prayers.

The more I study God's Word, the more I find it replacing my words and thoughts as I pray to God. It's not forced, religious, or ritualistic. I just find that his words as written in Scripture are alive and relevant in my life.

Learning how to pray should not be daunting. If you desire to seek God, he will show you how. The process is gradual, unforced, and led by the Holy Spirit. Like any good relationship on earth, seeking God shouldn't be repetitive and dull. Instead, it should be dynamic, evolving, and full of life.

3) Prayer is work.

Everything worthwhile in life is accomplished through discipline. In fact, the more important something is, the more discipline it requires, and nothing is more critical than prayer.

Donald Whitney, in his book *Spiritual Disciplines for the Christian Life*, writes: "I've seen Christians who are faithful to the Church of God, who frequently demonstrate enthusiasm for the things of God, and who dearly love the Word of God, trivialize their effectiveness for the Kingdom of God through lack of discipline."[51]

This is a tragedy.

In my experience, people who make a difference for God

---

51   Donald Whitney, *Spiritual Disciplines for the Christian Life* (Colorado Springs, CO: NavPress, 1991), 21.

are not necessarily talented or uniquely capable, but they are
dedicated to prayer.

My parents have lived extraordinary lives. They have faithfully
preached the gospel all over the world for forty years and have
had a hand in thousands of people coming to Jesus. It is no
exaggeration to say that God has used their lives to change the
world, and yet they are normal people. I believe this is because
they have authentic personal relationships with God and an
intense desire to know him better. My whole life, I have witnessed
their unwavering commitment to prayer, and I have no doubt
that this is the reason why God has used them so powerfully.

But prayer is work.

The apostle Paul was aware of the serious nature of prayer.
He didn't treat it casually but "labored" in it day and night. He
constantly spoke of the importance of seeking God and urged
the church to "strive" or "wrestle" in prayer.

For most of us, seeking God has become a dull ritual that
lasts for fifteen minutes in the morning. We need to understand
that prayer is our only weapon in the fight. Without it we are
powerless, and the enemy knows it. We need to fight *to* pray,
we need to fight *in* prayer, and it isn't going to be easy.

The good news is that discipline breeds desire. If you
commit yourself and refuse to give up, you will experience
incredible joy as your prayer life grows and your relationship
with God deepens.

4) This is war.

You may not know it, but there are spiritual forces trying to prevent you from praying. Have you noticed how tired you seem to get the very moment you decide to seek God? Or how quickly you become distracted?

Paul warns us that "we do not wrestle against flesh and blood, but against the rulers, against the authorities, against the cosmic powers over this present darkness, against the spiritual forces of evil in the heavenly places."[52]

Satan knows that if he can get us to focus on "flesh and blood" and ignore the spiritual battle we're in, then we'll be less inclined to pray. Prayer is our only weapon; if we aren't praying, we aren't fighting—it's as simple as that.

Adopting a "battle mindset" in prayer is crucial. Having this mentality means you expect things to be hard and aren't surprised by opposition.

The Bible describes the devil as a roaring lion looking for someone to devour. But there's good news. He who is in us is greater than he who is in the world,[53] and when we push through the obstacles and pray, God shows up. I have experienced this.

Another tactic of the enemy is to convince us that prayer does not produce real change.

------

52   Eph. 6:12.

53   1 John 4:4.

There have been times in my life that I have lacked the faith to believe that God can truly solve my practical problems, and so my prayers have become last-resort and filled with doubt. How is it that we can believe God created the universe and everything in it and yet lack the faith to believe he can provide for our most basic needs? As my relationship with God has grown, so has my faith and, along with it, my understanding that *only* prayer produces meaningful change.

Martin Luther, a seminal figure in the Protestant Reformation and an incredible man of God, once said, "I have so much to do today that I'm going to need to spend three hours in prayer in order to be able to get it all done."

We are often guilty of responding in the opposite way—praying less the busier we get. Worse still is being so busy doing things for God that we fail to involve him in the process, as if our effort, not his power, will make the difference. It all stems from the core lie that prayer doesn't produce *real* change.

In her blog, Elisabeth Elliot writes, "Pray when you feel like praying . . . Pray when you don't feel like praying. Pray until you *do* feel like praying."[54]

Prayer is nonnegotiable if we are going to change anything. Without it, we are simply outmatched—the problems are too

---

54   Elisabeth Elliot, "Notes on Prayer," *In His Strength* (blog), May 2nd, 2009, https://inhisstrength.wordpress.com/2009/05/02/notes-on-prayer-by-elisabeth-elliot/.

great, and our abilities are too limited. It's incredibly naive to think that we have the skills and resources required to make a lasting difference. What we do have is access to the Creator of all things, who is infinite in power, resources, and wisdom, and who inexplicably chooses to use us as a part of his plan. Realizing this changes everything!

3
THE MOTIVATION

The first time I went to Ukraine was on tour with No Longer Music in 2011. There was a clear hunger for the gospel there, and many people gave their lives to Jesus. Despite the fruit we saw, we dealt with many challenges, including corruption and economic instability, but we never felt unsafe.

That changed in the spring of 2014.

I had been invited to speak in three different cities in the eastern part of the country. A week before I arrived, political tensions between the pro-Russian Ukrainian government and those who wanted a deeper alliance with Western Europe boiled over. The whole world watched as thousands of protesters clashed with riot police. Buildings were set on fire, and many died. This event kick-started a major conflict between the two sides, and the resulting war continues today.

Given the circumstances, I wondered whether I would be able to go, but our local Ukrainian partners assured me it would be safe. It ended up being amazing but very intense, and I was exhausted by the end. On my way home, I took an all-night train to Kiev (the capital city of Ukraine) early in the morning.

Before heading to the airport, I walked around Maidan Square, the epicenter of the protest. Evidence of chaos and violence was everywhere. Rioters had torn bricks from the streets to throw at police, and barricades blocked the city roads. The smell of smoke still filled the air. It was a surreal scene.

A few years later, we went back on another No Longer Music tour of Ukraine. The mainstream news had stopped covering the conflict, but the fighting was still ongoing. We were confident that God had called us to go there, but I was anxious about driving back into a war zone.

I remember speaking with one of our local promoters a week before we left. He explained how he'd visited the church that would host the first concert of our tour. The church was in a city in the west of Ukraine, many miles away from the fighting and considerably more stable. He explained that after his meeting, he'd stepped outside and something hadn't felt right. It was strangely quiet, and the only people on the streets were riot police. He'd walked carefully to the train station and headed home, unsure of what else to do.

He'd later found out that a radical political group had driven up and down the streets shooting at people with automatic weapons and had stormed a government building. Local officials threatened to cancel our show. They feared that an outdoor, public event was simply too risky given the circumstances.

Valery, our local promoter, told me all of this one week before

JESUS IN THE SECULAR WORLD 71

we were supposed to do a show in this city!

As he explained how the "stable" parts of Ukraine were now violent as well, I felt a deep fear come over me. My wife was a few months pregnant, and we hadn't yet told anyone. I remember thinking, "It's one thing to go as a single guy into these places, but now I'm supposed to take my pregnant wife into a war zone? God, I'm not sure I can do this."

Over the years, I've been in many intense situations, and they haven't always been safe. I've had rocks thrown at me, fled from a riot in Lebanon, and been followed by the secret police. Once, our power was cut right before we were supposed to play. At a show in Albania, a guy threw a cell phone at my head while I was preaching.

When I got married, my wife joined No Longer Music, and we faced some dangerous situations together.

During one show, our stage was set up facing a mosque, and the local imam (a person who leads prayers in a mosque) confronted us while we were talking to people after the show. He was angry that we were sharing our faith. He got in the face of one of our bandmates and shouted, "Why have you come here? We are Albanians. We are Muslims. Why are you spreading these lies?"

We tried to calm him down, but he just got angrier. He gathered a large group of young men around him, and they began chanting, *"Allahu akbar"* ("Allah is the greatest"). Two policemen nervously stood between us and the mob and urged us to leave. They warned us that if the crowd became violent, there was nothing they could do.

We packed up as quickly as we could and prayed for God's protection. Fortunately, they didn't attack us, and we were able to drive away.

This incident shook me, and I remember feeling the weight of having brought my wife into this dangerous situation. Trusting God with my life was one thing, but trusting him with my wife required an entirely new level of faith.

People often ask, "Why would you risk going to war-torn Ukraine or Albania during Ramadan?" It's a valid question. If you're going to go to these kinds of places, you'd better have a good reason.

What I've learned is that before doing anything for God, you had better be clear about your motivation.

There would have been nothing noble about putting myself, let alone my pregnant wife, in danger for the sake of adventure or because "it was the right thing to do." Following God into precarious situations should have nothing to do with thrill seeking—it should be about having God's heart.

If prayer is the source of power for changing the world, then God's broken heart is why I even act in the first place. In fact, I would argue that if we do not love the lost, then we have no business trying to reach them.

So what does it mean to have God's broken heart?

In the parable of the lost sheep in Luke 15, Jesus shows us

exactly the kind of heart we should have. This passage has been instrumental in shaping how I've approached ministry, and it has had a profound impact on my relationship with God.

This parable begins by establishing the context.

"Now the tax collectors and sinners were all gathering around to hear Jesus. But the Pharisees and the teachers of the law muttered, 'This man welcomes sinners and eats with them.'"[55]

Sinners and tax collectors gathered to hear Jesus speak, and the religious elite were not happy about it. They did not mix with sinners—to do so was highly taboo—but Jesus rejected social norms. He didn't just spend time with sinners; he ate with them. This was unthinkable, because sharing a meal with someone in that culture was a very intimate act. In fact, Jesus spent so much time with sinners that the Pharisees accused him of being one himself, saying, "Here is a glutton and a drunkard, a friend of tax collectors and sinners."[56]

With this context in mind, Jesus says: "Suppose one of you has a hundred sheep and loses one of them. Doesn't he leave the ninety-nine in the open country and go after the lost sheep until he finds it? And when he finds it, he joyfully puts it on his shoulders and goes home. Then he calls his friends and neighbors together and says, 'Rejoice with me; I have found my lost sheep.'

---

55   Luke 15:1–2 (NIV).

56   Matt. 11:19 (NIV).

I tell you that in the same way there will be more rejoicing in heaven over one sinner who repents than over ninety-nine righteous persons who do not need to repent."[57]

This passage illustrates something critical about lost sheep: they're lost. That's why they're called "lost sheep." They aren't going to come to us, and we shouldn't expect them to. We need to follow the example Jesus set for us and go after them.

The good shepherd didn't get together with the rest of the flock and plan a big event, all in the hope of luring the lost sheep back home. No, Jesus says he went after the lost sheep.

We are often guilty of expecting non-Christians to come to us. We devise strategies and put together all sorts of programs, inviting the "outside world" to our home turf—but it rarely works. Jesus didn't spend the majority of his time in the synagogues or with the religious leaders but on the streets with everyday people.

A Battle of the Bands in the Middle East

Going after the lost sheep is hard because it forces us out of our comfort zones. In my life, it's often meant going to places I personally didn't like.

The 2009 No Longer Music tour had an unusual start. We were invited to be the judges of a heavy metal battle of the bands in Beirut, Lebanon. The event was held in a club called Tantra

---

57   Luke 15:3–7 (NIV).

(a name describing a superlative sexual experience). This was definitely a "lost sheep" place.

It took over twenty-four hours to travel to Beirut, and by the time we arrived we were exhausted. The next morning, we drove to Tantra and started setting up. From the moment I stepped into the club, I hated it. We were in the Middle East in the summer, so, needless to say, it was hot—very hot! Because there was no air-conditioning or windows, it was well over 100°F (38°C) inside. We had arrived at around two in the afternoon, but we didn't play until two in the morning.

While I'm not a huge metal music fan, I can appreciate the best bands in any genre. But these bands didn't even qualify as average—they were terrible! Nonetheless, I had to sit there for twelve hours, in 100°F+ temperatures, and judge—and judge I did. Although, I don't remember writing down any scores or comments. What I do remember is being miserable and wanting to leave.

When it was finally our turn to play, I was beyond exhausted, and I couldn't wait for the day to be over. The show started, and several hundred young Lebanese metal fans crowded in front of the stage, including a band from the Hezbollah part of town that had played earlier in the night.[58]

During our show, we theatrically depict the crucifixion and

58   Hezbollah is a Shi'a Islamist militant group and political party based in Lebanon.

resurrection of Jesus, and it's not uncommon for the spiritual atmosphere to change when we lift up the cross. On that particular night, not only did God's power fall on the crowd, but something in *my* heart began to change as well. I started to see the audience through God's eyes. When the show ended, my dad jumped off the stage, went into the middle of the crowd, and began to speak.

"You aren't here just to see a cool concert," he explained. "Jesus wants to break the chains. You aren't going to find freedom in your music, politics, or religion—the only way you can truly be free is if you give your life to him." He then asked if anyone wanted to give their life to Jesus.

A large group of Lebanese young people knelt in response to David's invitation. We formed a large circle and stood hand in hand, praying out loud, and we could feel the presence of God.

This was an amazing experience, and I remember feeling ashamed of my attitude from earlier in the day. This was the last place I would have chosen to go, and yet I had the privilege of experiencing God's power transform many lives that night. Though I felt unworthy, I could sense how pleased God was that we had been willing to go to this "lost sheep" place. At that moment, I understood clearly what Jesus meant when he said we should leave the ninety-nine to go after the one.

But how does the church typically react to places like Tantra?

Don't we say things like, "Thank you, God, that you will never see me or any of my friends in a place like that"?

So often, those of us in the church equate making a difference with taking moral stands and being a little better than those around us. We figure that if we swear less and avoid R-rated movies, we are making an impact. The truly "spiritual" among us join together to pray against places like Tantra, asking God to shut them down.

This brand of Christianity more closely resembles the religion practiced by the Pharisees than the dynamic, transformative life lived by Jesus. But following Jesus is so much more than a dead religion of dos and don'ts. As Eric Metaxas said, "Christianity is less about cautiously avoiding sin and more about courageously obeying the will of God."[59]

The Jesus of religion is dull, unattractive, and, most importantly, false. We shouldn't be surprised that the world rejects this version of Christianity. As pastor Matt Chandler of The Village Church says, "The least sexy version of Christianity in the universe is the one that says, 'Just be a better person.'"[60]

When we reduce Christianity to a book of rules or a program of behavioral modification, not only do we distort the gospel, but we also risk taking on the very pharisaical attitude Jesus strongly

59   Eric Metaxas, *Bonhoeffer: Pastor, Martyr, Prophet, Spy* (Nashville, TN: Thomas Nelson, 2010), 486.

60   Matt Chandler, "God the Protector and Defender" *The Village Church Resources,* June 12, 2016, https://www.tvcresources.net/resource-library/sermons/god-the-protector-and-defender.

opposed. Trying to "be better" only leads to self-righteousness, if we succeed, or despondency, if we fail.

Far from calling us to avoid dark places and sinful people, Jesus wants us to be in the middle of the mess and to share his love with those who need it most. If Jesus had lived in Beirut, Lebanon, he would have known about Tantra. He would have known the club's owner, the bartenders, and those who hung out there. If Jesus had spent time in New York or London, he would have known the drug dealers and the prostitutes, and he would have eaten with them.

Jesus dealt very seriously with sin, but he loved people. Why is it that followers of Jesus so often fail to follow his example? We treat the lost as if they are enemies—as if it's us against them—but they are the ones he came for (not to mention that we were once lost, too)! I believe it breaks God's heart when we distance ourselves from those who don't know him.

The good shepherd left ninety-nine righteous sheep behind to pursue the one that was lost. The parable says that when the shepherd found the lost sheep, he picked it up. This sheep wasn't clean. Like the prodigal son, it had made a mess of things. But the good shepherd was so overjoyed at having found what was lost, he didn't care—he put it on his shoulders and carried it home.

The world needs to see followers of Jesus who demonstrate this kind of extravagant mercy.

It's Going to Cost You

You might be thinking, "Alright. I have to go after lost sheep. I get it. On my lunch break or over the weekend, I'll take some time out of my busy schedule and go look for some. But I have a family, bills to pay, and a lot of responsibility, so I can't go that long. After all, I have to be reasonable about this, right?"

Reaching unbelievers is not another "good Christian task" to add to your list. When we think of it in this way, we miss the point. This isn't about religious duty or alleviating our guilt.

Let's go back to the parable for a moment. I like to imagine the whole scene being more interactive than how we typically read it. Picture Jesus explaining to the crowd how they should go after the lost sheep. At one point, one of the Pharisees, eager to prove his religious devotion, jumps in.

He says, "Okay, Jesus—fair enough. We need to leave the ninety-nine. But exactly how long should I be expected to look? A day? A week? Give me the required amount of time, and I'll fulfill my obligation."

Jesus responds in verse 4, saying:

"What man of you, having a hundred sheep, if he has lost one of them, does not leave the ninety-nine in the open country, and go after the one that is lost, until he finds it?"

How long should he look? *Until he finds it.* There is no time limit, nothing held in reserve, no backup plan—just total devotion to the lost sheep. This is another critical aspect of having the heart of the good shepherd. We must be willing to go after those who don't know God at great personal cost and sacrifice.

One of our band's key partners in Albania once said, "The devil comes after us full-time, so we cannot fight him as part-time Christians." This is the message Jesus is communicating with the parable of the good shepherd: we have to be all in!

You might be thinking, "So, I can't eat or sleep?" Of course you can. This is similar to Paul's challenge to "pray without ceasing." It's a hyperbole intended to communicate the intensity and devotion required to reach the lost. Jesus was fully committed to the will of his father. Having God's heart means being a little unreasonable and a little imbalanced in our concern for people.

For those who are married, think about how you felt the first time you met your husband or wife. In pursuing him or her, were you worried about your schedule or all the errands you had to run? Obviously not. You were falling in love. You discarded all other priorities and went after that person. That is the love-fueled, slightly out-of-balance, totally devoted pursuit that Jesus wants from you and me when it comes to his precious lost sheep.

You're going to need this kind of attitude, because it won't be easy. I'm only speculating, but it's possible the lost sheep didn't even *want* to be found. In fact, it may still have been running when the shepherd found it.

So what should our reaction be? If I were the shepherd, I would eat the sheep—that would teach it. At the very least, I'd tie a rope around its neck and drag it home. A little humiliation would do it some good.

But what does the good shepherd do? Jesus says that he picks up the lost sheep and carries it home. What a stunning picture of God's grace. We rebel; he pursues. We disobey; he carries us home.

This is the kind of heart we need: the heart of the good shepherd.

If we don't have God's broken heart for the lost, then our attempts to reach people will be cold and cliché: no more than rants on social media or meaningless bumper stickers. So often we think we're making a difference when we're not. We pick an issue and take a moral stand, but what is that accomplishing?

Take abortion, for example. Abortion is an unspeakable evil: routine genocide happening every day in our strip malls. But rather than reflexively speaking out against this horrific tragedy, have you gone to God in desperate prayer? Have you wept over the staggering and callous destruction of human life? Have you asked him to show you how to respond?

What about the desperate women who feel so terrified and alone that they choose to end the lives of their unborn children? Do we really care about them? Until we allow God to take our theological concerns and turn them into deep, personal anguish, our efforts to reach people will be harsh and powerless.

The secular world perceives Christianity as a religion of dos and don'ts. They only know us for the things we oppose.

As David Kinnaman observes, "Outsiders think of our

moralizing, our condemnations, and our attempts to draw boundaries around everything. Even if our standards are biblical, they seem to be all we have to offer."[61]

We are always crusading against the evils we see in the world, but where's our compassion? Where's our mercy? To reach the secular world, we need to have the heart of the good shepherd. Sadly, we too often act like the Pharisees rather than Jesus, and this needs to change.

How Can I Change My Heart?

No matter how hard we try, we cannot make ourselves have God's heart. It's not about willpower. It won't work to say, "Starting tomorrow, I'm going to love people."

If I'm honest, my natural inclination is selfishness. On good days, I might care about the needs of my closest family members and friends, but even that doesn't come easily. Unfortunately, this is the default setting of the human heart, and sheer willpower is not enough to overcome it. So what can we do?

We can repent and say, "Lord, I don't care about people the way I should. I need you to change me."

And this isn't a one-time thing. We need to develop a posture of repentance, especially as it relates to this, because overcoming selfishness is a lifelong battle. It is possible, however, to grow in

---

61   David Kinnaman, *unChristian* (Grand Rapids, MI: Baker Books, 2007), 52.

this area. Though I still struggle, I have seen that when I humble myself before God, he changes me.

The Bible makes it clear that God loves an honest and humble heart. In the wake of his greatest moral failure, King David says, "A broken and contrite heart, O God, you will not despise." [62]

Over the years, I have experienced God's love and compassion for the lost, and it is overwhelming.

A few years back, No Longer Music played in a Polish prison. We were supposed to do our show outside on a big stage built especially for us by the inmates, but on the day of the concert it was raining, and we were forced to change our plans and relocate to a small room.

This particular prison had nearly two thousand inmates, and we'd hoped most of them would come, but instead only a handful of them crammed into the tiny space given to us. The concert was stunningly bad. Our "stage" was only a few feet wide, and most of our equipment wouldn't fit inside the room. We performed as best we could, but it was a mess. Despite the circumstances, several of the prisoners prayed with us afterward to receive Jesus. We took comfort in the fact that it wasn't an entirely lost cause.

The next year, we were invited back, and this time the weather was perfect. Again, we had been promised a big wooden stage,

---

62   Ps. 51:17.

and, sure enough, it was built by the time we arrived. The chaplain warned us that many famous bands had performed at this prison, and it wasn't uncommon for the inmates to show little interest.

Contrary to our expectations, seconds into our first song, around five hundred inmates rushed towards the stage, clapping and cheering. It was just like any other concert—well, apart from the machine guns, barbed wire, and guard towers.

When we started to show how Jesus died and rose again, we could feel the atmosphere change. David jumped off the stage and spoke to the audience. He explained, "God is a good father. He is not an alcoholic or an abuser. He loves you and proved it by sending his son, Jesus, to die for you so that you could be free!"

As David was talking, God's presence came over the prison so strongly that it felt like a physical weight. David pointed at the biggest, toughest-looking inmate and said, "God loves you." The prisoner stood there, clenching his jaw and holding back tears. In that moment, he seemed to be a boy again—free to accept God's incredible love. The whole experience was surreal.

David went on. "I know that in prisons there are rules. If you respond to messages like this, you could get beat up—but I think some of you are tired of feeling empty inside. Today, you can be free. If you want this freedom, you have to kill your pride and raise your hand in front of everyone here."

Over fifty men responded to the gospel. We were all blown away. I remember packing up our equipment in a daze. The shock of God's palpable love lingered, and even our non-Christian sound crew was amazed by what had just happened. It seemed as if a grenade had gone off.

I have been to more churches than I can count, but I have never felt the love of God more strongly than I did in that prison. When I tell the story even now, years later, I experience God's overwhelming love just as I did on that day. But it wasn't because of something I did. My part was being willing to go; but it was God who broke my heart.

See, Feel, Do

Often, we don't have God's heart because we just don't see the needs around us.

We keep our doors locked, drive to work, avoid deep conversations with strangers or colleagues, have our close circles of Christian friends, and stay away from the "bad" neighborhoods—out of sight, out of mind.

A commercial showing starving children in Africa or the sight of a homeless person on our drive home might temporarily provoke an emotional response, but then we change the channel or look the other way. I know this is true, because it's what I have done.

If you are feeling convicted and are eager to respond, trying harder will not work. The solution is as simple as it is difficult. You need to submit to the prompting of the Holy Spirit, admit honestly before God the condition of your heart, and ask that he will do in you what you cannot do for yourself.

After that, there are some practical steps you can take, the first of which is pretty simple: just open your eyes. Of course, the "seeing" transcends your physical eyes and is largely about the heart, but there is still a practical component to this advice. It's much harder to ignore what is right in front of you.

As we start to see, we start to feel.

Henry David Thoreau famously wrote, "The mass of men lead lives of quiet desperation."[63]

People don't go around announcing their brokenness, but don't be deceived: they are hurting and desperately in need of hope.

You have to be willing to step outside your comfort zone and enter into the suffering of others. Once you do, God will change your heart and use your life to make a difference.

Like so many things in life, this is not a one-time thing. We need to *continually see, feel, and do.* Right action is always preceded by right thinking. As Paul says, "Don't be conformed to the patterns of this world, but be transformed by the renewing of your mind."[64]

One pattern of this world is to care only about our own needs. Paul challenges us to push beyond ourselves and to share Jesus

---

63   Henry David Thoreau, *Walden* (Boston, Massachusetts: Ticknor and Fields, 1854), 8.

64   Rom. 12:2.

with a world that is desperate for answers.

God's devotion to the lost is undeniable. Luke 6 describes how heaven throws a huge party when a person surrenders to Jesus. We need this kind of heart if we are going to reach the secular world for him.

If our hearts are not broken, our efforts will have no impact. But this concern for others is not something that we can manufacture; it's a gift that God gives freely to those who ask.

I have no doubt that God wants to use your life to reach the secular world for him. But if your efforts are not fueled by his power and motivated by his love, they will not produce fruit.

4
CLOSE THE GAP.
SPEAK THE RIGHT LANGUAGE

Over the last ten years, I have shared the gospel in some of the most unreached countries in the world, and I have witnessed an incredible hunger for Jesus. I am convinced that there is a sincere and growing desire for the truth in secular culture. The problem is not a lack of interest, or the gospel itself; the problem is that we Christians have become irrelevant.

The perception among vocal atheists is that the "God question" is not as much contentious as it is unimportant. They suppose that science has replaced our need for a deity and that most modern people have just lost interest in spiritual things altogether. However, my experience has proven the opposite to be true.

Have you heard it said that Christians answer questions people aren't asking, or that they speak a language that the world doesn't understand?

How did this happen?

The simplest explanation is that we stopped interacting with the "real world" and retreated to our religious subcultures. Not surprisingly, we have lost touch with and become foreigners in our cities.

When it comes to relevance, *isolation is our enemy.*

We Christians have secluded ourselves to varying degrees throughout history. Perhaps the most obvious example is the monks of medieval Europe, who removed themselves from culture altogether, believing this to be the only way to remain uncorrupted.

Much of our inability to communicate with secular culture today is due to similar, albeit more subtle, versions of the monastic isolationism of our Christian past. Our modern seclusion is less overt, but it is a problem nonetheless. We may interact with secular people in superficial ways, but our interactions with them are rarely meaningful.

Over the years, we have justified our cultural distance in different ways, including a well-meaning but misguided attempt to create Christian alternatives to mainstream entertainment.

This initiative has led to a Christian version of everything: books, movies, music, etc. I'm not suggesting that we shouldn't have Christian entertainment, but I think we have inadvertently created a fear-driven mentality. The result of this has been a generation of believers who have distanced themselves from the world altogether.

Authentic Relationships

Like Jesus, we need to be present in secular culture rather than hide from it. But relevance is much deeper than entertainment and fashion; it's about having authentic relationships with nonbelievers.

As Tim Keller says, "Have friends who are not just Christians."[65] It's really that simple.

In my experience, Christians often have very few, if any, meaningful relationships with secular people. This is a problem. Most of us are surrounded by non-Christians at work, at school, or in our neighborhoods. Needless to say, these would be good places to begin to develop real relationships.

Depending on your personality, this may seem daunting, but you don't have to do it alone. Ask God to guide you. Over the years, I've prayed, "Lord, whom have you put in my life who needs to know you?" God will answer that kind of prayer. But as I've already mentioned, this cannot be taken on as a project. It's not about adding something to your to-do list.

Our goal should be to develop *authentic* relationships. Doing so will meet the arguably greatest-felt need of the secularized world: community.

---

65   Keller, Timothy (@timkellernyc). 2016. "Having a public faith means not retreating into Christian subculture. Instead have friends who are not just Christians." Twitter, August 24, 2016, 2:30 p.m. https://twitter.com/timkellernyc/status/768515730803392512.

The Western world is experiencing a loneliness epidemic. According to a 2016 survey, 72 percent of Americans report feeling a sense of loneliness.[66] The breakdown of the family and the rise of social media are among the causes, but the point is that people today are lonely and crave real relationships.

Several years ago, I experienced a short season of loneliness that gave me a taste of how intense it can be.

I was halfway through college and was supposed to be experiencing the social pinnacle of my life. But my first attempt at friendships hadn't gone particularly well, and I found myself having to start over. Until that point in my life, I'd always had great friends, so this was a new experience for me.

I spent many weeknights and weekends walking on a path in front of the old folks' home near my apartment, praying. My prayers were angry and filled with frustration. I didn't understand why I was in this place. It was a difficult time, but God taught me a lot through it.

One thing was clear to me: we are not made to be alone. Genesis 2:18 says, "Then the Lord God said, 'It is not good that the man should be alone; I will make him a helper fit for him.'"

God declared this before man's fall, and it was the first time he

66   Survey Finds Nearly Three-Quarters (72 Percent) of Americans Feel Lonely," *The Harris Poll*, 2016, https://theharrispoll.com/a-new-survey-of-more-than-2000-american-adults-found-72-percent-report-having-felt-a-sense-of-loneliness-with-nearly-a-third-31-percent-experiencing-loneliness-at-least-once-a-week-the-survey-was/.

said that something was "not good." This is important, because it means our hunger for relationships is not the result of weakness or sin, nor is it the by-product of biology; rather, it is a reflection of having been made in the image of God. As a follower of Jesus, my need for community is validated in who I am.

Contrast that with the dominant worldview today: secular humanism. This prevailing mindset reduces relationships to being a means to an end. It's all about serving my needs. Concepts such as self-sacrifice, deference, and service are foreign. Secularism has elevated personal autonomy and pleasure-seeking to the highest place, leading to rampant consumerism, individualism, and isolation. Add to that virtual relationships, social media, and a constant flood of entertainment, and you're left with people who've been deceived into thinking they no longer need real connections, despite experiencing immense loneliness.

We are desperate for genuine relationships, and yet we increasingly operate from a worldview that undermines community-building structures and behaviors—and it's killing us. According to a recent study conducted by global health service company Cigna, "Loneliness has the same impact on mortality as smoking 15 cigarettes a day, making it even more dangerous than obesity."[67]

---

67   Cigna U.S. Loneliness Index, *Survey of 20,000 Americans Examining Behaviors Driving Loneliness in the United States*, May 2018, https://www.multivu.com/players/English/8294451-cigna-us-loneliness-survey/docs/IndexReport_1524069371598-173525450.pdf.

As followers of Jesus, how do we respond to the lethal loneliness in our world?

Once you begin developing authentic relationships with non-believers, you should *ask questions and listen*. This might sound a little remedial, but it's rarer than you might think. In our highly individualized, self-focused world, genuine friendships are uncommon.

There was a joint study done at Duke University and the University of Arizona; it consisted of 1,500 face-to-face interviews. One in four people interviewed said they had no one to whom they could talk about their troubles or triumphs. When family members were taken out of the equation, this percentage doubled, to include more than half of the interviewees.[68]

Loneliness is killing us, but we are not without hope. God not only provides a basis for community, but he is also sympathetic to the millions who lack it.

There are lonely people all around you who are desperate for someone to invite them into their lives, serve them, and listen to them.

Our hearts should break for the lonely people all around us. Genuine community and friendship are extremely attractive to a relationally starved, secular world. Followers of Jesus should

---

68   Janice Shaw Crouse, "The Loneliness of American Society," *American Spectator*, May 18, 2014, https://spectator.org/59230_loneli-ness-american-society/.

recognize this need and see it as a tremendous opportunity for the gospel.

To be clear, I am not suggesting a bait-and-switch approach to developing relationships. Pursuing a friendship with an unbeliever must never be a ministry strategy; it must be motivated by a genuine desire to know and love that person. It will be obvious immediately if our concern is a facade rather than a real demonstration of love.

Relevant Language

Jesus was relevant because he had an intimate understanding of the culture and people of his day. His parables were not only incredibly creative and insightful but also consistent with the people and places he was reaching out to. He spoke of sheep and shepherds, sowing and seeds, and making fishers of men. These weren't randomly chosen, abstract illustrations—they were vivid images that spoke directly to his audience.

Inspired by biblical examples, many Christians take the specific language used by Jesus and apply it directly to their particular context. We declare, "Jesus is the good shepherd!" This was powerful imagery in first-century Israel, but today? Obviously not. And yet we are often guilty of this very thing.

There are many well-meaning followers of Jesus who sincerely want to share the gospel but who are ineffective because they are using outdated and unhelpful "church language." This oversight in communication is costly, because many secular people are open to the gospel but simply don't understand what we are trying to communicate.

We have to become aware of our "in-house" terminology and discard anything that wouldn't make sense to someone without a church background.

Consider the following explanation of the gospel:

In Genesis, we learn that God created the universe and everything in it. But Adam and Eve were deceived by Satan, who convinced them to eat the apple from the tree of life, even though God had told them not to.

They both gave in and disobeyed God, and the result was the fall of all humanity. But God made way for us to know him again by sending Jesus to earth. Jesus came, died, and rose from the grave. He took all of our sins on himself, and if we accept what he did, we will be saved, go to heaven, and spend eternity in his presence.

Now, compare that with how I might share the gospel with a non-Christian after one of our evangelistic concerts.

Every day, you are told lies. When you watch TV, when you go online, at school, at work—all day, every day, all you hear is lies. The world tells you that you're an accident—the result of an explosion in the sky. You are nothing more than a highly evolved animal.

Because of these lies, you chase after things that will never satisfy you. No matter how many possessions you have, no matter how many vacations you take or parties you go to, it's never enough.

You don't have to live this way. You don't have to believe these lies.

You are not an accident. You were created by God, and he isn't far away. He is not an impersonal life force. He is not an abusive or alcoholic father but a good one.

We were made to have a relationship with God, but there is a problem. The world is broken, and we're all to blame. Every day, I do things I don't want to do. I hurt myself and those around me. And it doesn't matter how hard I try; I keep doing things I don't want to do—a sense of guilt haunts me.

The reality is that the bad things I do separate me from God, and if you're honest, you're like me.

But there's good news! God didn't leave us without hope. He sent his son, Jesus, to earth, and he wasn't wealthy or famous. He was with the poor, despised, and rejected. Jesus fed the hungry and healed the sick, but most importantly, he took the punishment we deserve for the bad things we've done.

The only thing that gets in the way of us seeing Jesus is our pride. We have to let go of control and receive what he has for us. He's reaching out his hand—all you have to do is grab on, and he will pull you up. If you say to him with an honest heart, "Jesus, I need your help and forgiveness, I want to surrender to you," he will hear you, and he will come into your life!

Notice the difference?

The obvious difference is in length. This is necessary because explaining the gospel in a way that avoids presuppositions and is accessible to the nonreligious requires more words.

Beyond that, the difference is in the specific phrases I use and the assumptions I make.

First, I don't use the Bible as a mutually agreed upon source of truth. Doing so assumes that the person I'm talking to views Scripture as more than literary fiction—which is unlikely in secular culture.

Second, I don't assume the person believes he or she needs the gospel. Instead, I focus on the logical implications of an atheistic worldview. I think that all people share common longings and desires, so I address those specifically. Everyone longs to be valued. Except for the most militant nihilist, no one lives as though life has no meaning. No one wants to believe that life is merely about gaining material things, growing old, and dying, and yet a purely naturalistic worldview leaves us with little alternative. Highlighting this bleak reality opens the door for the gospel to be heard and received.

Next, I explain who God is, but without referring to the Bible. Instead, I use words and imagery that a nonreligious person can understand. I describe God as a good father. Many young people grow up in broken homes with absent fathers. The promise of a father who loves them and is there for them is compelling to those who have never experienced this.

I then turn to the problem: our sin. But I don't use the word "sin." Instead I say, "The bad things we have done." This might seem overly pedantic, but the difference is important. Not only is "sin" a confusing word in our culture, but it also carries with it a lot of misconceptions. By contrast, everyone understands and nearly everyone accepts that we've all done bad things. I have learned that whenever I can use a nontraditional way of explaining a concept without losing its original meaning, I should.

After that, I offer the only solution: Jesus. Many secular people think that if God does exist, he doesn't care about us. Jesus's life proves the opposite to be true. To make this point, I emphasize how he fed hungry people and healed the sick. Most importantly, I explain how he forgave us and made it possible for us to know him.

Finally, using normal, everyday language, I explain how we can accept what Jesus did for us.

The differences between these two explanations of the gospel might seem trivial, but I have seen a significant difference in how they're received. Of course, this doesn't guarantee people will accept the gospel. As I've repeatedly said, this isn't about methodology or our powers of persuasion. Rather, it's about eliminating any unhelpful church language that impedes secular people from seeing and accepting the *real* Jesus.

We need to reintegrate into secular culture and eliminate the superficial differences that keep us isolated and irrelevant. Jesus's life demonstrates a delicate balance: being part of culture while not being polluted by it. There is a significant risk if we go too far in either direction. Jesus doesn't want us to conform to our culture, but he doesn't want us to live completely separately from it either.

So let's get out of our Christian ghetto, develop authentic relationships with unbelievers, ask them questions, and really listen. It may seem simple, but the impact of doing this will be huge.

5
SHOW THEM WHO JESUS IS

Speaking the right language is the first step to reaching the secular world for Jesus. Next, we need to show them who he is.

If I were to go into a secular club or workplace, stand on a table, and shout, "I am here in the name of Jesus," it's likely no one would listen—and not just because they would think I had lost my mind. This approach would be ineffective because most unbelievers have an inaccurate perception of Jesus. Common culprits are popular media, adverse experiences with Christians, and simple ignorance. Regardless of the reason, the Jesus they reject is one you would also reject.

To get beyond people's misconceptions, I have learned that we need to *show* people the gospel, and then *tell* them. Your approach will vary greatly depending on your calling and context, but there are some universal principles we can all follow.

In No Longer Music, we use art and music to demonstrate the life, death, and resurrection of Jesus. We depict the gospel in a nontraditional way. We avoid using overly religious symbolism or imagery, without distorting the message. In our performance, a character who represents Jesus creates a guy and a girl. The guy he creates ends up abusing the girl. The Jesus character then picks the girl up and carries her to the front of the stage, drops to his knees, and weeps.

This scene is critical because we are starting to "show" people Jesus. Many non-Christians think that if God does exist, he doesn't care about their pain.

Our No Longer Music performance speaks directly against this lie. The truth is that God's love for us is beyond measure. He cries over our suffering, and we use our performance to show this in a vivid way.

At the end of our performance, the Jesus character sacrifices his life for the girl so she can live. He is killed on stage and then comes back to life. We take the audience on a powerful journey of sacrifice, redemption, and reconciliation. Though the audience might not be aware, what they have just watched is the gospel.

The show ends with these lines:

The sick song goes on and blind we dance to its beat.
We are chained like slaves, caught in a lie, can't you see?
We are more than what they say we are
An explosion in the sky without meaning,
A mutated animal without feeling,
A cosmic freak of chance,

No Purpose, No Plan.
It's time to disconnect;
It's time to meet the Ultimate Life Force.
The One who breaks all the chains,
The One who loved us all along.
And His name is *Jesus*.

Our show is an hour long, but not until the very last line do we even say "Jesus." We do this because we want our audience to "see" the gospel before they hear it. By depicting the life, death, and resurrection of Jesus in a modern way, we create the space for people to experience God. Most secular people have heard the gospel many times, but not many have actually understood it. This is why we try to *show* them and then *tell* them.

We have performed this show all over the world, and the impact is incredible. I've had countless conversations with people who say things such as, "I'm not supposed to like this religious stuff, but I understand this message, and I feel the power in what you're showing."

Sadly, it's rare for the gospel to be presented in a way that makes sense to nonreligious people. By taking the time to "show" people who Jesus is, you're able to bypass their walls and misconceptions. This isn't simply some academic theory I've developed; it's something I have seen played out in real life. As part of No Longer Music, I have "shown" people who Jesus is hundreds of times all over the world, and I have had the privilege of seeing thousands of people respond to the gospel.

During a No Longer Music tour of Russia, we were experiencing pressure from the government not to preach. In one city in the southern part of the country, Rostov-on-Don, we were working closely with a local church that had been inspired to organize a show partly because they had read my dad's book *Rock Priest*.

On the day of our concert, a nationalistic militia showed up. They told our manager they were against anything American or European, and they planned to shut us down. Despite the threats against us, David felt we needed to preach.

A crowd of around three thousand people came to the show, and they were immediately engaged and enthusiastic. When it ended, David began to speak, and, while most listened, a few in the crowd started shouting. I found out later they were yelling things such as, "Go home, Americans!" and, "You can't talk about Jesus here!"

Despite the tense atmosphere, David explained the gospel. He then invited those who wanted to have a relationship with God to come forward. The local church estimated that two hundred people prayed to receive Jesus that night. After the show, I talked to a guy named Max. He seemed really touched, and I asked him what he thought of our message. He said that the performance gave him a "totally new understanding of God." He explained that he'd had a basic idea about God, but had "locked it up deep inside a box in his soul."

Max shared that after watching our show, he felt ready to "take it out of the box and look at it again." I asked him if he'd received Jesus at the show, and he said he had. I was able to pray for him and then connect him with a local church.

Our depiction of the gospel created the space for Max to reconsider a false idea he'd had about God and to accept Jesus for the first time.

Let me be clear again that reaching people is not about having the perfect approach or strategy. Persuasive words will never change a person's heart—that is the work of the Holy Spirit. Yet Jesus clearly modeled taking the time to communicate in a relevant way.

Jesus was capable of an overwhelming display of supernatural power at any time. He easily could have used his power to convince people who doubted him to believe—yet he didn't. Why? I believe it's because he wanted people to choose him freely. Real love always involves choice. If I had the power to *make* my wife love me and used it, that wouldn't be real love. At times, Jesus did reveal his supernatural power, but often he reasoned with people and allowed them to decide. His life modeled the principle of *showing* truth before outright speaking it.

I have seen that only God's power changes lives, and yet sharing truth in a creative way is a critical part of effectively demonstrating who Jesus is to a lost world. Specifically, I have seen that art is one of the best ways to demonstrate the heart and character of Christ to the secular world today.

The Power of Art

Human beings are always building, inventing, and creating. Much of what we've built is for survival: houses to protect against the elements, weapons to conquer or defend, machines that help us move more quickly and efficiently. Over time, we have become better at surviving, but we go beyond simply surviving: we create. We make art. Have you thought about how unusual that is?

From a purely naturalistic perspective, there are few good reasons to make art. It serves no practical function, and yet we have always created it. It seems to be in our blood. Why?

As a follower of Jesus, the explanation is obvious. Our universe is the handiwork of an extraordinary artist. Consider the complexity of the cellular world, the uncountable number of stars and planets, the brilliant diversity of species, the breathtaking landscapes, the power of the ocean, and the vast nothingness of the deserts. God designed the world and everything in it, and human beings are his masterpiece.

Christians believe that God made human beings unique from all other created things. He endowed us with his image, and, because of this, every living person has inherited characteristics that connect him or her with the divine. One such connection is the innate desire to create.

So we write stories, paint paintings, and sing songs, and this God-given desire to create has immense power in communicating truth. The fall corrupted this gift, as it did everything else, and as a result, art is often shallow and self-focused. In reaction to the destruction that is so often caused by art, many Christians have chosen to devalue it altogether and therefore miss out on its incredible power to produce change. This has led to the myth that art doesn't have, or doesn't need to have, a message. Yet art is always saying something. It's not a matter of whether you will communicate a message; it's about what message you will communicate. Good art wrestles with the big questions and challenges the status quo.

Picasso's *Guernica* vividly depicts the horror of the Spanish Civil War, and it brought attention to the largely unnoticed brutal dictatorship in Spain. Billy Holiday's "Strange Fruit" is based on a poem that recounts witnessing a lynching in the American South. This song, along with many others, helped fuel the civil rights movement. John Lennon's "Imagine" reflected a growing frustration over the division in society caused, in his mind, by nationality and religion. This song profoundly affected the millions who heard it, and its impact is still felt today.

Art changes things and is as relevant today as it has always been. Young people aren't looking to their parents or pastors for guidance; they are turning to online stars, musicians, and other celebrities. Today's famous artists have armies of impressionable fans. Their influence is enormously powerful.

Throughout my life, I have seen evidence that art is an incredible tool for conveying truth.

You may be thinking, "That's great, but I'm not an artist."

Don't be so sure.

Being an artist is not limited to playing an instrument, nor is it characterized by some arbitrary standard of ability. It's not even about whether you're making a living doing it. Talent, hard work, or commercial success can indicate if someone is a "successful" artist, but not whether he or she *is* an artist.

I'm not sure many would consider Jesus an artist. Vocationally, he was a carpenter, yet he was also a brilliant storyteller. His parables were not only rich and imaginative but also compelling and relevant. He modeled the power of art in communicating truth to secular people.

The mind is drawn to story, and story is incredibly effective in conveying a message. Consider the parable of the prodigal son, one of most famous stories in all of history and a great example of the power of art.

As the story goes, this son demanded his inheritance and went "into the far country." He spent all his money on "reckless living" and found himself "longing to be fed with the pods that the pigs ate."[69] The son reaped what he had sown and found himself in the lowest place imaginable—envying pigs!

He then came to his senses and chose to return home, hoping to be taken in as a servant. Remarkably, when his father saw him, he "felt compassion, and ran and embraced

---

69   Luke 15:13,16.

him and kissed him."[70]

What a stunning picture. The father didn't wait for his disobedient son to make the slow, shameful walk back home; instead, he ran to him and threw a giant party to celebrate his return. Jesus could have just said, "I am compassionate and merciful. If you turn to me, I will forgive you," but this would not have communicated the message with the same effectiveness as his story.

Art is a powerful tool because it bypasses our defenses. In 2 Samuel 12, David commits adultery by sleeping with Bathsheba, Uriah's wife. To cover his tracks, he has Uriah murdered.

Despite his actions, David is unrepentant. Nathan the prophet knows of the sins David has committed, but he also knows that confronting him directly will not work, so he uses a story to expose him.

He tells of a wealthy man, who has a large flock of sheep, and a poor man, with only one little ewe. When a traveler comes into town as a guest, the rich man takes the poor man's ewe to feed the guest, instead of using one of his many sheep. In response to this, David says, "The man who did this deserves to die!" In a brilliant turn, Nathan replies, "You are the man!"[71]

At that moment, David recognizes his wrongdoing and is devastated. Nathan's approach bypasses David's self-deception

---

70   Luke 15:20.

71   2 Sam. 12:5–7.

and leads to his genuine repentance and to his famous confession in Psalm 51:16–17, where he says, "A broken and a contrite heart, O God, you will not despise."

If Nathan had tried to confront David without using an illustration, it's likely David would have ignored him or worse. This story acted as a mirror, allowing David to see his own heart in a manner that could not have been accomplished through direct communication.

Art can speak in a way that words simply cannot. For this reason, it is critical that we encourage and celebrate art as a powerful way to communicate truth.

There simply aren't enough Christian artists using their creative gifts to communicate truth outside of the church.

This may seem way out of your comfort zone, but I believe God would give you a creative way to show people who he is, if you asked him. I'm not suggesting you quit your job and become an artist. I'm asking you to consider the people God has put in your life and to ask him to show you how you could communicate the truth to them in a way that would penetrate the walls and lies that surround their hearts and blind their eyes.

I believe God wants to use you in an artistic way to share the truth.

Perhaps your way of showing Jesus to someone is to point them to a gifted artist who already does this. Or maybe you use a work of art as a conversation starter. It could be a beautiful painting, a compelling video, or a song that illustrates a powerful truth about God.

The art doesn't need to be Christian at all. I have found that truths about God and the nature of reality are often embedded in secular works of art.

In August 2017, the rapper Logic released a song with the unusual title "1-800-273-8255." It turns out this is the number for the American National Suicide Prevention Lifeline. The song and its video went viral. The song reached number three on the Billboard charts,[72] and the Suicide Prevention Lifeline reported receiving a staggering 4,573 calls the day the song was released.[73]

In interviews, Logic expressed his desire to tell a story that could reach people in need and let them know they weren't alone.[74]

---

72   Gary Trust, "Logic's '1-800-273-8255' Is Now Highest-Charting Phone Number in Hot 100 History," *Billboard*, September 18, 2017, https://www.billboard.com/articles/columns/chart-beat/7966064/logic-1-800-273-8255-highest-charting-phone-number-song.

73   Megan Armstrong, "Logic Tweets National Suicide Prevention Lifeline Statistics Since His '1-800' Release," *Billboard*, November 16, 2017, https://www.billboard.com/articles/columns/hip-hop/8039094/logic-1-800-273-8255-national-suicide-prevention-lifeline-statistics-tweet.

74   Jen Yamato, "Inside Logic's Grammy-nominated suicide prevention video, with Don Cheadle, Matthew Modine and a mission," *LA Times*, January 26, 2018, http://www.latimes.com/entertainment/music/la-et-ms-grammys-hip-hop-logic-1-800-music-video-don-cheadle-20180126-story.html.

This is an excellent example of the power art has to generate attention for a desperate situation and to bring real change.

I have personally experienced the unsettling power of art. I remember the first time I saw the 2004 movie *Crash*. It weaves together several plots, looking at issues of identity, gender, and race in the aftermath of 9/11. Having grown up in many different countries, I had always considered myself sensitive to the racial dynamics around me. Yet this film challenged the superficial nature of my understanding, bringing to light the severity of the problem, and it continues to have an impact on me to this day.

Art is a gift from God and a powerful tool. I have watched cynical young people all over the world brought to tears as my band depicts the life, death, and resurrection of Jesus on stage. I have seen God unleash his power through our videos, music, and movements and transform lives in ways that leave little doubt about the unique role of art in reaching the secular world for Jesus.

Outward Evidence of Inward Transformation

In Matthew 5:13, Jesus says: "You are the salt of the earth. But if the salt loses its saltiness, how can it be made salty again? It is no longer good for anything, except to be thrown out and trampled underfoot" (NIV).

Salt enhances flavor, and, in a similar way, following Jesus should enhance life. Christians, on the other hand, are often considered dull and lifeless. Why is this?

It is either a misconception or a sad indication that many Christians simply aren't living in light of what they claim to believe.

The secular world sees Christianity as a list of rules that limit human freedom and take the fun out of life. Yet the opposite is true: God created all good things, and we should be the freest people of all.

Still, any parent knows that freedom without boundaries is not in our best interest. My son is certainly free to run across the road without looking, but doing this will likely get him killed. We quickly learn that many of our desires are destructive and need to be resisted. Gratifying all of our immediate impulses never leads to true joy.

The fullest life is found in obeying God. I have experienced that the closer I am to him, the freer I become. This is because he created me, the world, and everything in it. He has a design for every aspect of my life, and he can be trusted.

The world parades its rebellion against God, and people are being destroyed. True joy and fulfillment can be found only in knowing God and following his design. The life of a genuine follower of Jesus should radiate authentic joy, and this is attractive to a world that only experiences counterfeit pleasure.

I believe we underestimate the testimony of a life well-lived, and this is part of showing people who Jesus is.

As Christians, our actions speak volumes to the world around us and critically affect how people see Jesus. Our lives should not look like everyone else's, but often they do. Why should a secular person want to follow a God who is powerless to change us?

When I was nineteen years old, I spent a semester studying in Europe with a group from my university. I was arrogant and had a lot of growing up to do.

At one point, I was on a train heading to Austria and talking to one of the girls in our group. I was telling her about my desire to travel the world and use art and music to tell people about Jesus. She stopped me in the middle of a sentence and said, "How can you want to be a missionary? You don't love people."

I was stunned. This was coming from a very genuine, caring person. I was upset, but not angry. Honestly, I couldn't argue with her.

All these years later those words still ring in my head. She was right. I knew the truth, but my heart was cold. Since that day, I have prayed a thousand times that God would soften my heart and help me to love people as he does. I have asked him to close the gap between what I know and how I live.

As followers of Jesus, we need to take our actions and attitudes very seriously and realize that Christian hypocrisy is a major barrier to reaching secular young people. Studies have shown that there is little difference between the behaviors of professing

Christians and of those who claim no religious beliefs at all.[75] Worse still are the "Christians" in our culture who say and do awful things that in no way reflect the teachings and character of Christ. These modern-day Pharisees may represent only a small percentage of believers, but they tend to be the most noticeable. Sadly, in the eyes of secular culture, they speak for the rest of us.

One night while driving home, I was listening to a national sports radio show. The hosts were talking about the terrible things that are said on Twitter.

They were discussing the "commenting" phenomenon when one of them said, "You know the funniest part? You'll be reading the worst, cruelest hate-filled tweet and then you'll read the person's bio and inevitably it will say 'Loving father of three and follower of Jesus.'"

They laughed, and all agreed this was a common experience. As I listened, I felt ashamed.

This isn't right. We serve a God of power. It is impossible to have an intimate relationship with God and remain unchanged, so why is it that so few Christians live like Christ did?

How should we respond to accusations of Christian hypocrisy today?

I am aware that much of the secular perception of our hypocrisy lies in a misunderstanding of the gospel. Our behavior

---

75 Kinnaman, *unChristian*, 47.

does not save us; salvation is a gift we cannot earn. Thankfully, we aren't asking people to follow us.

Our message is this: "Grace has rescued me, and I have been made new. Although I will fail along the way, over time I will look more like Jesus." We can profess this message with confidence because, in Christ, we know who we are. As Matt Chandler often says, "The good news of the gospel is hypocrites are welcome."[76]

We live with the inescapable fact that there will always be a gap between the radical obedience to which we are called and how we actually live.

Armed with the proper understanding of the gospel, we can get on with the job of becoming more like Jesus in action and attitude, in service and love, while knowing that failure is part of the process. By God's grace, we can come to peace with the fact that our lives are inching ever closer to a goal that we will never fully achieve on this earth.

This is a radical idea when compared to all other world religions.

Every belief system other than Christianity teaches that our salvation depends on our behavior. Jesus preached a radically different message. He taught that our actions would never be enough and that he had to do for us what we could never do for ourselves.

And yet, there's a certain tension. Paul addresses this apparent

---

76   Matt Chandler, "Delightful Discipline," *The Village Church*, November 11, 2012, https://www.tvcresources.net/resource-library/sermons/delightful-discipline.

paradox in his letter to the Romans. In chapter 5, he explains how God entered into human history through his son, Jesus, offering the final atoning sacrifice for all humankind. He argues Old Testament law was introduced to demonstrate man's sinfulness and to highlight God's glory, which culminated in the final work of Jesus on the cross.

He then poses a critical question in chapter 6, verses 1–2. "What shall we say then? Are we to continue in sin that grace may abound? By no means! How can we who died to sin still live in it?"

When Jesus died on the cross, something extraordinary happened: we died with him. Paul tells us in 2 Corinthians 5:17: "Therefore, if anyone is in Christ, he is a new creation. The old has passed away; behold, the new has come." This is great news! It means that we are no longer slaves to our earthly desires. God has delivered the decisive blow to our sinful nature and supplied us with the power of the Holy Spirit to live out a new life as new beings. This is an awkward "two steps forward, one step back" dance. We will never be without sin while in our earthly bodies. Nevertheless, there should be outward evidence of an inward transformation.

James, the brother of Jesus, famously said, "Faith without works is dead."[77] This doesn't mean our works save us, but rather that they are evidence that our faith is real.

In the same way, if we claim to believe in God but our lives show no evidence of this belief, something isn't right. If we are

---

77 James 2:26 (NKJV).

going to "show" the world who Jesus is, we have to start living in such a way that demonstrates that following him is more than a powerless tradition. If people can see the impact of the cross at work in our lives before we speak, it will give us great authority when we do.

One time after a No Longer Music concert, a city official came up to our manager. He had a puzzled look on his face and said, "Your team . . . they work so hard and yet it is so clear that they love each other. How is this possible? If our government operated like your band, this would change our country!"

Our manager reported this back to us, and we were amazed by the impact that our team's unity was having on those around us. Of course, we don't always get it right, and we daily rely on each other's mercy and God's grace, but it is clear that if God is living inside us, people should notice.

Be Merciful

Showing people Jesus means focusing on people, not on sin. What separates believers from unbelievers is not the absence of sin, but rather the acknowledgment of it and the acceptance of grace. Before I surrendered my life to Jesus, I was blind to the truth. I lived in darkness because I didn't know there was light.

Paul puts it this way in 2 Corinthians 4:4: "The god of this age has blinded the minds of unbelievers, so they cannot see the light of the gospel that displays the glory of Christ, who is the image of God" (NIV).

We need to recognize that those who do not yet know God are deceived and are acting apart from a true understanding of his will. This distinction is critical, because it will affect how we treat secular people. It can sound obvious, but we cannot hold them to a standard they are unaware of. Yet often that is exactly what we are doing.

Jesus doesn't expect people to be finished products; he focuses on the heart before dealing with the behavior. When asked why he was spending so much time with sinners, Jesus replied, "It is not the healthy who need a doctor, but the sick. I have not come to call the righteous, but sinners to repentance."[78] We are called to rescue people, not to stand back and point out their sin.

Jesus models what a merciful heart looks like in John 8. In this particular story, a woman is caught committing adultery. The Pharisees bring this woman before Jesus in the temple courts. Imagine the humiliation of having your sins on display in public.

In this time period, adultery was a capital offense, and public shaming for such a crime was typical. To our modern minds, this seems unthinkable, but back then, it was common for offenders to be exposed and executed. This particular case was unusual, though. The Pharisees not only intended to shame and ultimately stone this woman—they were also using her in a ploy to trap Jesus.

---

78   Luke 5:31–32 (NIV).

From the very beginning of Jesus's public ministry, he broke all the cultural and religious rules. He ate with sinners, spoke with prostitutes, and rebuked the self-righteous. The religious establishment hated him, and this instance of the woman caught in adultery was their latest attempt to get rid of him. They were aware of his reputation for showing mercy, but it was clear that Jesus also knew the Mosaic law—so what would he do? Forgive the woman? Or uphold the law and allow her to die?

Not surprisingly, Jesus isn't caught off guard, and his response is brilliant.

He invites those without sin to cast the first stone.[79] Only God is without sin, and the religious elite wouldn't dare compare themselves to him in this way. To do this would be to commit a sin far worse than adultery. All the woman's accusers leave, and then she is left alone with Jesus.

The Pharisees didn't care about this woman at all. Their intentions were to use her as a ploy and then kill her—nothing more. Jesus covers her shame and drives away her accusers. He bends down and, in a breathtaking display of mercy, asks her a simple question: "Woman, where are they? Has no one condemned you?"[80]

She responds, "No one, Lord," and, in the midst of the

---

79   John 8:7.

80   John 8:10.

woman's terrible shame and guilt, Jesus offers her a way out, saying, "Neither do I condemn you; go, and from now on sin no more."[81] How sweet those words must have sounded.

Notice that Jesus didn't ignore the sin that this woman had committed. The message of this story is not "Everyone sins, and Jesus is cool with it." After all, he commands her to leave her life of sin; but *first* he shows mercy.

We are never told whether this woman truly changed. For all we know, she went back to her life of sin, but I suspect that having received such extraordinary grace, she was never the same again. This remarkable example provides a blueprint for how we should treat those who do not know God.

In dealing with people, Jesus modeled the same pattern throughout his ministry: go after the heart, and the behavior will follow. He was patient and kind with sinful people, and we need to follow his lead.

Religion leads to death, but Jesus leads to life. Religion is human-made and self-seeking, but Jesus breaks down the walls and levels the playing field. With Jesus, there are no religious elite. We are all sinners in need of a savior.

The world sees Christians taking plenty of moral stands, but it doesn't see us showing mercy enough. This perpetuates a false Jesus and leaves the lost in darkness. The Bible warns us

---

81   John 8:11.

that we will receive mercy only if we show it. Perhaps we need a revelation of just how much grace we need on a daily basis. Just as he did in the parable of the debtor, Jesus has wiped away a debt so large that we should never be able to demand to be paid back what is owed to us.

Our lives should demonstrate the transformative power living inside of us. Our attitudes and actions are not the gospel, but there is power in a life that shows the gospel first and then speaks it.

The world thinks it knows who Jesus is, but it doesn't. As his followers, we must show people who he is. We must ask God for creative ways to demonstrate his heart. The secular world needs to see that God is not far away, angry, or disinterested. He doesn't demand mindless obedience; he is the basis of all rational inquiry. He's the source of beauty, the author of creativity, and the only source of real joy. Secular people need to see who the real Jesus is, and it's our job to show them.

6
REMOVE THE BUSHES THAT OBSCURE THE CROSS

If I had gone out on the streets of any American city fifty years ago and asked people questions such as, *How did we get here? What's the meaning of life? Is there such a thing as right and wrong? and What happens when we die?* I could have expected most people to give similar answers.

For most of American history, Christian theism was the dominant worldview. Of course, not everyone had a genuine, personal relationship with Jesus, but the basic tenets of the Christian faith were accepted by virtually everyone.

For example, it would have been normal to use the Bible as a source of moral authority outside the church, or to speak publicly about heaven or hell.

This simply isn't the case anymore.

We live in a post-God society where young people don't see God or the Bible as sources of authority. What's more, they believe morality is relative, and that heaven and hell are not likely to be real.

Given this reality, we can no longer approach the doubts and questions of nonbelievers with "the Bible says it, and that settles it." That time has come and gone, yet Christians today have been slow to realize that our view of the world is increasingly out of step with those outside the church. We think we have more in common with people than we actually do.

Becoming relevant begins with taking a step back from our assumptions and finding common ground with those we are trying to reach. In technical terms, this is called presuppositional apologetics, and understanding what it is and how to use it is vital if we are going to reach the secular world for Jesus.

You might be thinking, "Isn't apologetics for intellectuals who like arguing?"

Not necessarily. It's essential that we avoid defining apologetics too narrowly. After all, apologetics just means defending a particular position. For most of us, apologetics evokes an image of two people talking back and forth with no hope of changing each other's minds. It's easy to see where this perception comes from, because this is what we observe in nearly all of the "Christian versus atheist" debates found online.

It's important to understand that these debates are intended to influence the thousands, if not millions, of people listening—and not necessarily the two people debating. Certainly, the debaters hope to change each other's opinions, but their primary goal is to persuade their audiences, who are often unsure and seeking out answers to these critical questions.

We shouldn't be intimidated by the highly academic and technical proficiency of professional debaters. There are those who have the ability to defend Christianity at a very high level, and I thank God for those people, but everyone should be able to defend their faith to some degree.

I am convinced that, if viewed correctly, presuppositional apologetics can be a powerful tool in reaching people for Jesus.

Here are a few reasons why.

Defend Our Hope

The first reason is to defend our hope. 1 Peter 3:15 says, "But in your hearts honor Christ the Lord as holy, always being prepared to make a defense to anyone who asks you for a reason for the hope that is in you; yet do it with gentleness and respect."

Atheism is a bleak worldview. That alone doesn't make it untrue, but a world without transcendent purpose or meaning doesn't exactly inspire hope. Richard Dawkins famously said, "The universe we observe has precisely the properties we should expect if there is, at bottom, no design, no purpose, no evil, no good, nothing but blind, pitiless indifference."[82]

In light of this perspective, how does an atheist cope?

For most of them, the secret lies in not thinking about it. Human beings have an extraordinary ability to ignore

---

82   Richard Dawkins, *The Blind Watchmaker* (New York, NY: Norton, 1996), 133.

inconvenient realities. We numb our doubts with busyness and pleasure, mask our frailties with pills and seatbelts, and seem shocked by death. Without God, there simply is no way to make sense of our chaotic, fleeting existence—so we don't even try.

A godless reality doesn't offer much hope, but until a person is forced to confront the logical outworkings of this perspective, he or she may go on blissfully ignorant for years. In reality, a world without God is dark and desperate.

By contrast, Christian theism is full of promise! 1 Peter 3:15 highlights the reality of our hope found in God and our need to explain it.

Perhaps the greatest potential for demonstrating the strength and resilience of the Christian faith lies in times of suffering. Christians believe that God created all life and endowed it with unique value. Our sin brought suffering and death into the world, but God restored the mess by sending his son, Jesus, to rescue us. By placing our faith in him, we will receive the gift of eternal life as well as comfort, guidance, and love during our time on earth. In light of this, we can endure hardship knowing that God cares, our pain matters, and one day everything will be made new. A follower of Jesus is not immune to hardship but has the perspective and hope to overcome and move forward.

How are atheists supposed to make sense of suffering? After all, without God we are just victims of an indifferent universe. As Richard Dawkins puts it, "DNA neither cares nor knows.

DNA just is. And we dance to its music."[83]

I have been extremely fortunate to have experienced very little personal tragedy, but I have heard countless examples that powerfully illustrate the resilience people can find in Christ.

A few years ago, I was reading about a pastor and his family. While he was working out, three men broke into his home and murdered his pregnant wife.[84] There are no words that can adequately describe just how evil this act was; I could barely take it in. As a dad and husband, I'm not sure I could go on living if this happened to me.

People may argue about the existence of objective morality, but even the most callous intellectual would view this as unequivocally evil.

How was this pastor supposed to respond? No one would blame him for hating those men, and certainly no one would expect him to forgive them—yet his response was stunning.

In a statement released by his church, he wrote: "I hold firm to the belief that God is still good, that He takes our tragedy and

---

83   Richard Dawkins, *River Out of Eden: A Darwinian View of Life* (New York, NY: Basic Books, 1995), 133.

84   Niraj Chokshi and Michael E. Miller, "Suspected killer of pastor's wife, 'watched her bleed,' court document says," *Washington Post*, November 23, 2015, https://www.washingtonpost.com/news/morning-mix/wp/2015/11/23/ind-police-arrest-teen-for-rape-murder-of-pastors-pregnant-wife-amanda-blackburn/?noredirect=on&utm_term=.0c077a92f661.

turns it into triumph, and that the best truly is yet to come."[85]

How is this possible? Where does the strength come from to be hopeful in the darkest of circumstances? The only explanation lies in our access to the unending depths of God's peace and presence. I love thinking about Paul and Silas with their hands and feet chained down, locked up in the "inner prison," singing worship songs at the tops of their lungs—this is the kind of strength the world cannot explain.[86]

When we, as followers of Jesus, are not only able to endure but to thrive in the darkest of times and in the darkest of places, we will point to superhuman resilience that demands an explanation.

I remember learning about Corrie ten Boom in school. Her family hid Jews from the Nazis during World War II, and eventually they were caught and thrown into a concentration camp. Her sister died, but Corrie survived.

Life in the camp was a horrific ordeal, and they suffered more than most of us can imagine. Many years later, Corrie tells the story of her experience at a church in Munich, where her former guard from the concentration camp asked her to forgive him. To make matters worse, he was no ordinary guard—that would

---

85   Kelly Ledbetter, "Pregnant pastor's wife fatally shot in home robbery," *Christian Examiner*, November 13, 2015, https://www.christianexaminer.com/article/pregnant-pastors-wife-fatally-shot-in-home-robbery/49790.htm

86   Acts 16:25.

have been bad enough. He was the cruelest and most sadistic of them all.

After the war, he had given his life to Christ and had prayed for years that he might meet someone from the camp so that he could ask forgiveness for the terrible things he had done. Corrie described how at first she was unable to forgive him. "That moment I felt a great bitterness swelling in my heart. I remembered the suffering of my dying sister through him."[87]

But then she felt moved by God, and said, "At that moment a great stream of love poured through me, and I said, 'Brother, give me your hand. I forgive all.'" She said afterward to the man who had watched this exchange, "You never touch so much the ocean of God's love as when you love your enemies."

Unbelievable!

How can a person imprisoned for preventing genocide, a person who was stripped, beaten, and starved, choose to forgive one of the people responsible for her suffering? The truth is that following Jesus equips us not only to endure pain, but also to overcome it. Why? Because the Christian worldview is hopeful.

In Jesus, every person has been forgiven a debt far beyond his or her ability to repay. Jesus commands us to forgive others because he forgives us, and he empowers us to forgive even those who may seem unforgivable.

---

87   Corrie ten Boom, *Tramp for the Lord: The Story that Begins Where The Hiding Place Ends* (Fort Washington, PA: CLC Publications), 82.

Faith in God grants us a supernatural hope, no matter how horrific our circumstances might be. In the midst of the hell of a Nazi death camp, Corrie ten Boom wrote: "No matter how deep our darkness, He is deeper still. He not only rose from the dead, He changed the meaning of death and therefore of all the little deaths—the sufferings that anticipate death and make up parts of it. He is gassed in Auschwitz. He is enslaved in the Sudan. He's the one we love to hate, yet to us He has chosen to return love. Every tear we shed becomes His tear. He may not wipe them away yet, but He will."[88]

Life is not meaningless. Evil is not an illusion, and neither is good. Horrible things happen in this life, but one day God will restore all things. Moreover, we will all be held accountable for how we lived. In God, there will be justice.

Equipped with this view of the world, we should be able to live with deep joy and a sustained hope. 1 Peter 3:15 is claiming that how we live and how we suffer will stand in sharp contrast to the world, and they will want to know how we do it. So let's defend our hope!

Unfortunately, defending the Christian faith doesn't come effortlessly. Peter says we must be prepared. Your belief in God may help you to be well-equipped to cope with the world, and your hopefulness may be evident for all to see. Are you ready

---

88   Lee Strobel, *The Case for Faith* (Grand Rapids, MI: Zondervan, 2000), 52.

to make a good defense?

Follow Biblical Examples

The second reason we need to become effective Christian apologists is to follow biblical examples.

It's clear from Scripture that Jesus was an apologist. He took the time to communicate the truth persuasively. He was able to find common ground with his audience by using illustrations and imagery that aligned perfectly with the culture of his day.

A great example of this is found in John 10:3, which says: "The gatekeeper opens the gate for him, and the sheep listen to his voice. He calls his own sheep by name and leads them out" (NIV). This would be a strange illustration for an American today, but it made perfect sense to a first-century Israelite. Sheep jargon would have been relevant vernacular.

The shepherd's job was to protect and guide the sheep. Over time, they would learn to recognize his voice. Jesus's audience would have instantly connected with the idea that Jesus was *the* shepherd calling them to follow him.

Jesus modeled the importance of establishing common ground with our culture to communicate a truth about God. Whether interacting with the religious elite, a Roman soldier, a despised Samaritan, or his own disciples, Jesus knew how to speak their language and how to reason with them. He dealt with their ignorance patiently. He understood their unique resistance to belief and was able to speak directly to their hearts.

The apostle Paul was another great apologist. His life demonstrated his devotion to engaging his culture in a relevant way. Acts 17:2–3 says: "And Paul went in, as was his custom, and on three Sabbath days he reasoned with them from the Scriptures, explaining and proving that it was necessary for the Christ to suffer and to rise from the dead, and saying, 'This Jesus, whom I proclaim to you, is the Christ.'"

Later, in verse 17, we see how Paul "reasoned in the synagogue with the Jews and the devout persons, and in the marketplace every day with those who happened to be there."

The ancient Far East included an intense mixture of religions and worldviews. You had Roman polytheism, Greek mythology, and the various sects of Judaism, along with general paganism and superstition. To reason with anyone who happened to be in the marketplace or synagogue was no easy task, but that's what Paul did.

We see Paul at his apologetic finest in Athens. Greek culture in this day was a confluence of rationality, science, and polytheism. The Athenians were especially committed to new ideas, so much so that Acts 17:21 describes how "all the Athenians and the foreigners who lived there would spend their time in nothing except telling or hearing something new." Debating new ideas was part of daily life, and so they welcomed Paul's perspective.

He addressed the Athenians and immediately demonstrated an understanding of their mindset. The Greeks were highly committed to appeasing their pantheon of gods. In fact, just to cover all their bases they created an altar "to the unknown god."[89] Paul saw this as an opportunity to share the gospel and said, "The God who made the world and everything in it, being Lord of heaven and earth, does not live in temples made by man, nor is he served by human hands, as though he needed anything, since he himself gives to all mankind life and breath and everything."[90]

Had Paul decided to save time and use the same approach he used with the Jews or the Gentiles, it's hard to imagine his words would have been as fruitful. By tailoring his message to the Athenians, he connected with them in a powerful way, and lives were changed. Many gave their lives to Jesus and said, "We will hear you again about this."[91]

The examples of Paul and Jesus alone should persuade us of the importance of apologetics. They both knew the culture and were able to engage with it with incredible effectiveness. We must follow their example.

Still, there's a tension worth mentioning. Paul certainly believed in discussion and dialogue, but he also said, "For I decided to know nothing among you except Jesus Christ and

---

89   Acts 17:23.

90   Acts 17:24–25.

91   Acts 17:32.

him crucified."[92] On the surface, this can seem contradictory. Paul leaves little doubt that it's the work of God's power through the Holy Spirit that changes hearts.

He says in 1 Corinthians 2:4, "My message and my preaching were not with wise and persuasive words, but with a demonstration of the Spirit's power" (NIV).

Like it or not, the Christian faith has many mysteries and apparent contradictions. Only God's power can bring about real-life transformation, yet Jesus, Paul, and others in Scripture clearly reasoned with people. We will never fully understand how our efforts to influence and persuade interact with God's power to bring about change in people's lives.

Following Jesus does not guarantee us a perfect understanding of all things—that would make us God. We often have to accept our limitations and live with what can seem like competing ideas. We must learn to become relevant while never forgetting that only God's power, not persuasive words, can change someone's heart.

Guard the Truth

The third reason why we need to be effective Christian apologists is to guard the truth.

All day long we are lied to. In science class, we are told that the

---

92   1 Cor. 2:2.

universe is the result of a cosmic explosion that happened billions of years ago and that our lives are a product of blind chance. Human beings are not special, just highly evolved animals. Some philosophers tell us that life has no transcendent purpose. We are here for no reason, and one day everything will cease to exist. Morality is a social construct, and all one can hope to do is avoid pain, acquire material possessions, and experience as much pleasure as possible.

In light of this perspective, Christianity is written off as naive and anti-intellectual. The New Atheists scoff, "Haven't we moved on from such childish superstition?"

The rational validity of the Christian perspective has come under severe attack. We are given a false dichotomy: science and reason on one hand, faith and fairy tales on the other. You either view things from a religious perspective or an academic one—the two share no common ground.

It's no wonder that people aren't taking Christian theism seriously when forced to choose in this way.

But this dichotomy is patently false. There are literally thousands of brilliant defenses of the Christian faith written by men and women from every academic field. The diverse range of contributors to Christian apologetics is one of its great strengths.

As followers of Jesus, we need to refute the notion that believing in God is irrational and unscientific in the public sphere.

I have been greatly encouraged by the work of Christian

scholars. I am grateful for historians who labored meticulously to prove that Jesus really walked the earth, claimed to be the son of God, was crucified at the hands of the Romans, was buried, and rose from the dead, leaving an empty tomb. By any academic standard, the evidence for these claims is virtually beyond refutation.

Christian physicists, as well as secular ones, have shown the universe to be so finely tuned that to suggest it came about from random chance proves how far into the realm of fantasy atheists are willing to go to defend their presuppositions. Biologists have poked so many holes in Darwinian macroevolution that if believing it wasn't vital to secular humanism, it would have been jettisoned long ago.

My point is this: if perception is reality, then atheism has won. The belief of secular people is that religion has no rational basis. It is thought that science has triumphed in proving religion's irrelevance and that the mature thing to do is accept that God may have played a role in the past but that Nietzsche is right— God is dead—so let's grow up and move on.

Sadly, many Christians have succumbed to the lie that believing in God comes at the expense of reason. This idea has driven many followers of Jesus underground. Fearing that their faith would fail if tested, Christians often prefer to keep their views private, hidden from the scrutiny of science and reason.

Paul asserts the exact opposite in Romans 1:20: "For his invisible attributes, namely, his eternal power and divine nature, have been clearly perceived, ever since the creation of the world, in the things that have been made. So they are without excuse."

The physical universe does not disprove God; it proclaims his existence! We are commanded to love God with all of who we are—our minds included. God breathes life into every rational and scientific inquiry. God is not afraid of our questions, our doubts, or our explorations.

God and science are not in opposition. God grounds, fuels, and, in fact, commands that we explore all that he has made.

How Do I "Do" Apologetics?

My first exposure to apologetics was in 2008 at the Steiger Missions School, when a local pastor gave a two-day lecture comparing Christianity with other major worldviews.

Listening to him explain and defend Christian theism using reason was very eye-opening. I had been a follower of Jesus most of my life, but I had never heard anything like this before. My faith was genuine, but it was based more on my emotions and experiences than on my intellect. These two days brought to life the commandment Jesus gave in Matthew 22:37: "You shall love the Lord your God with all your heart and with all your soul and with all your mind."

For the first time, I started loving God with everything I had!

This experience was just the beginning of what would become a lifelong pursuit. Apologetics, like any skill, is not going to be learned in a two-day seminar. Similar to working out or playing an instrument, mastering apologetics takes consistent effort over an extended period of time.

Getting started can, of course, be intimidating, but here are some guiding principles to help you.

1) Understand the Secular Mindset

This has been one of the primary themes of this book, and it's worth talking about again. We have to know the people whom God is calling us to reach; this principle applies regardless of the tools you employ.

We don't want to be "carpet-bomb" apologists. This approach pays little attention to the specific needs and language of an audience, and instead haphazardly covers anything and everything related to the Christian perspective. Doing apologetics like this communicates a greater interest in what we know than in the person we are trying to reach.

John Stackhouse makes this point in *Humble Apologetics*: "In a rapidly pluralizing and already widely diverse society, we must speak to people as they are, not just trot out our '20 sure-fire answers to 20 common questions'. To do so will mean listening and learning so that we can truly understand people's needs and pressure points, and the common ground on which we can then communicate what we have to give them in Christ's name."[93]

---

93   Stackhouse, *Humble Apologetics*, 161.

Good apologetics has more to do with listening than speaking. It's more about asking questions than about making statements. If you're doing most of the talking, you're doing it wrong.

Focus on asking questions—you'll be surprised by how much people open up. When interacting with nonbelievers, we can spend years tiptoeing around serious subjects. After all, people aren't willing to talk about God, right? This is a false assumption, and we are far too cautious. I have seen over and over that people want to discuss in-depth things if given the opportunity. We all share universal longings and experiences. Like you, secular people go through hard times and want answers to questions:

What's the point of my life? Does my pain matter? Where will I go when I die? Who decides what's right and wrong?

I have presented these types of questions to people in all sorts of different contexts, all over the world, and rarely, if ever, are people unwilling to answer.

And when you ask secular people questions, you begin to understand them. False assumptions erode away, and you will start to see real people with genuine struggles.

You may not have all or any of the answers at first, but that's okay. This will force you to go looking for them, and in doing so, you will strengthen your faith. In my experience, a sheltered, unchallenged worldview won't last, but if it's tested in the real world of competing ideas, it will thrive.

But first we need to really know people.

2) Compare and Contrast

A critical component of apologetics is demonstrating the logical fallacies and contradictions of the secular mindset and comparing this perspective with the coherent Christian worldview.

Along with asking questions and listening, a "compare and contrast" method works well, I've discovered. Comparing the secular perspective with the theistic one and allowing the contrast to speak for itself is remarkably effective—more so than repeating slogans.

There are two major tests to determine the validity of a worldview: coherence and correspondence. The strength of a worldview is judged on its internal coherence (whether or not its various tenets are logically consistent) and on how well it corresponds to reality. Christian theism scores high in both respects, especially when compared to atheism. Highlighting the contrast is a key goal of apologetics.

In my experience, it's not that people don't care about the metaphysical questions; it's that they haven't thought deeply enough about them to formulate coherent answers. Exposing the logical implications of the secular perspective can be very eye-opening and can be a powerful way to reach people outside the church.

After a No Longer Music concert in Bulgaria, I went out into the crowd and was immediately drawn to this one guy. He hadn't responded to our invitation to receive Jesus, but he still seemed interested in talking, so I asked, "Do you believe there is such a thing as right and wrong?"

"Yeah, I guess," he replied.

"Okay. But who decides what's right and what's wrong? Do you?"

"Yes. I think we all get to decide for ourselves."

"So, what if I decide that it's OK to kill children? As crazy as that sounds, if I believe that it's not wrong, is that okay?"

Shocked, he fired back, "No! Of course not!"

"Why?" I asked. "I thought we all got to decide for ourselves?"

Sensing the dilemma, he somewhat sheepishly replied, "Well . . . because . . . it's wrong!"

It dawned on him that something wasn't adding up. There had to be more than just human opinion involved in determining what was objectively right and wrong.

The conversation was very positive, and at no point did it become heated. I merely highlighted how his view of morality lacked internal consistency and failed to correspond with what he experienced in real life. Simply put, his worldview failed the test.

Another time, I was talking to a woman at a wedding. I don't remember how the conversation took a turn, but before we knew it we were discussing religion. She said, "I believe all religions are the same. I don't see any need to elevate one over another."

This is a prevalent secular perspective. Have you seen the bumper sticker that cleverly spells "coexist" using the symbols of different world religions? Well-intentioned as its creator may have been, the message being communicated is utterly incoherent.

It's tantamount to asking someone for directions to her house and having her reply, "I don't believe in one direction—take any route and you'll get there in the end." This illustration is, of course, ridiculous, but analogous to the affirmation "All religions are the same."

So I asked this woman at the wedding, "Do you believe that all religions are the same?"

"Yeah, basically," she replied. "I mean, the differences are pretty insignificant."

I pushed back. "Let's take three major world religions: Christianity, Judaism, and Islam. You're saying they teach the same thing?"

"Yeah, the important stuff anyway."

"I guess I'm confused," I said. "From my understanding, Christianity says Jesus is the son of God and that there is no other way to be saved except through him. On the other hand, Islam says Jesus was a prophet, not the son of God. In Judaism, Jesus was neither God nor prophet. These aren't minor differences. One must be true, or all of them must be wrong, but all of them cannot be right."

"Hmm. I guess I never thought about it like that."

I sensed an open door to share the gospel. Although she didn't give her life to Jesus on the spot, I could tell she was much closer than she'd been before.

When I defend Christian theism using reason, I'm after a "hmm" moment—an instance of clarity that creates an open

mind that allows me to present the gospel. It's not about humiliating someone or being right; it's about carefully removing
the false foundations upon which many people's beliefs rest.
The goal is to get the person to consider the rational flaws of
secular humanism while highlighting the rational basis for the
Christian faith.

I've seen God work powerfully through many of the "compare
and contrast" conversations I've had. Not all of them end in
life-altering epiphanies, and often people I've talked to leave
unconvinced—and that's okay. It's God's responsibility to change
people's hearts, and it's mine to know the truth and to gently
share it with those who will listen.

3) Address Barriers to Belief in God

Many people don't passively reject belief in God; they are
actively opposed to him. In their minds, there are strong reasons
for rejecting Christianity entirely. Typical reasons include the
problem of evil and suffering, Old Testament ethics, Christian
hypocrisy, and the science and faith dichotomy.

As followers of Jesus living in a pluralistic society, we have
to address these barriers to belief in God. We cannot ignore or
minimize them, even if we believe they are false. The human
experience is confusing and complicated. We are very limited
in our ability to understand how God operates in the world.
With this in mind, we need to be patient with nonbelievers who
wrestle with doubt.

Fortunately, Christianity has been defended by an exhaustive list of supremely gifted men and women. Moreover, as previously mentioned, Christian theism is remarkably coherent and corresponds with reality unlike any other religion or worldview. Because of this, we don't have to shrink back in the face of criticism. There are good answers to the objections raised against following God.

Take the problem of evil, for example. Like it or not, evil and suffering are part of the human story.

In light of this, a common objection to God is that since evil exists, God cannot be all-powerful and good at the same time. If God were good, he would want to stop evil, and if he were all-powerful, he could—so why doesn't he? Either God is good but not all-powerful and thus incapable of stopping evil, or he is all-powerful and not good and so chooses not to intervene. Given this impasse, many secular people conclude that God cannot exist—at least not the Christian God of the Bible.

There is a good response to this objection.

The truth is that love without choice is not love at all. If my wife had been forced to love me, would that love have been real? Obviously not, because a genuine relationship is freely chosen.

God created human beings, not robots, and in doing so he accepted the risk that we could decide to reject him. This allowed us to experience a real relationship with him. Ultimately, we chose to rebel against God, and this decision brought evil and suffering into the world.

If you accept the premise that God is real, and that evil and suffering are also real, then this explanation makes a lot of sense. But when it comes to evil and suffering, people are rarely rational—and this is understandable. Suffering is a deeply personal issue, not merely an academic one. Because of this, we must be very sensitive. Though it is not easy, it is possible to address the problem of evil by showing that true love requires a choice— our choices, not God, produce evil in the world.

Our greatest argument against an indifferent, unjust God is the cross. The cross shows that he is not indifferent, as he sent his son, Jesus, to earth to restore the brokenness we caused. He shared in our suffering and provided a path to redemption and healing. God did not create evil, but through Jesus he defeated it.

Another typical barrier is the science and faith dichotomy.

The common secular perspective goes something like this: "You either believe in myths and fairy tales, such as God, or in evidence, facts, and science."

This perspective is presented as a fork in the road. You must choose one; you can't have both. The consequences of this lie are severe. If you accept this dichotomy, then faith in God is indeed blind. You are forced to ignore any questions or curiosities you may have, and you simply must concede that faith and science are mutually exclusive—that to embrace one is to reject the other.

For atheists, this means that life's major questions don't merit serious consideration, and any transcendent longings or deeper meanings are illusory. Life is reduced to empiricism, test tubes, and lab results. This reductionist view of life may be popular in secular lecture halls and in pop-culture books on atheism, but very few people live as if this actually were true.

The truth is that science and faith are not contradictory. In fact, modern science owes a tremendous debt to Christ-following men and women whose beliefs didn't inhibit their scientific explorations but fueled them.

In fact, rationality and an ability to trust in our "knowing" is best grounded in the idea of a transcendent mind that created a rational, intelligible universe for us to discover. The uniformity of the laws of nature and the staggering regularity that we see all around us are best explained as the work of an intelligent creator, and they provide the necessary foundation for making scientific discovery possible.

As C.S. Lewis points out, "Men became scientific because they expected law in nature, and they expected law in nature because they believed in a lawgiver."[94]

This transcendent foundation launched some of the greatest scientific minds in all of history, including Newton, Galileo, Mendel, Pasteur, and Kelvin. Johannes Kepler, the renowned seventeenth-century mathematician and astronomer, described his motivation for discovery in this way: "The chief aim of all investigations of the external world should be to discover the

---

94   C. S. Lewis, Miracles: *A Preliminary Study* (London: Collins, 2012), 110.

rational order which has been imposed on it by God, and which he revealed to us in the language of mathematics."[95]

In any case, why would positing God as cause for the existence of the universe in any way limit our ability to "do science"? I am confident that Steve Jobs and Steve Wozniak created the Macintosh computer. If I decide I want to discover every aspect of their creation, my awareness of its creators in no way limits or cheapens my pursuit of that knowledge. This objection confuses ontology (the study of being) with epistemology (the study of how we come to know something). The truth is, God invites us to explore and discover the universe and everything in it.

There are many more objections to belief in God, including apparent atrocities in the Old Testament and supposed scriptural support of sexism and slavery. These barriers must be taken seriously, but all can be dealt with and explained. Again, the goal here is not to "win" an argument or to prove how smart you are. The goal is to create an unobscured view of the cross.

I once heard it said that, "Apologetics is not the cross, but it's the shears that remove the bushes that obscure the cross." Gently dealing with the barriers and obstacles people have to believing in God is exactly that—clearing the weeds so people can see who God really is.

---

95   Johannes Kepler, "De Fundamentis Astrologiae Certioribus," *Thesis XX* (1601).

4) Bring the Conversation to the Gospel

Paul was a brilliant apologist, and yet he recognized that persuasive arguments produce nothing apart from God. He wrote in 1 Corinthians 2:4, "My speech and my message were not in plausible words of wisdom, but in demonstration of the Spirit and of power."

Ultimately, for any apologetic conversation to produce fruit, it must include an explanation of the gospel. Often my best arguments have no impact, while the simple truth of the cross changes everything.

This is the point Paul was making when he said, "For I resolved to know nothing while I was with you except Jesus Christ and him crucified."[96]

I have seen this principle in action during my time in No Longer Music. We work all year round to improve our performance, and we rehearse full-time for a month before the start of a tour. We try to be as professional as possible, and yet often God moves most powerfully when we perform most poorly.

Once we played a show in Slavonski Brod, Croatia. We had no idea that David's book *Rock Priest* had been printed and distributed all over the country, and that the impact had been enormous. As a result, a local church offered to organize a national tour there. We agreed to come, and everywhere we

---

96   1 Cor. 2:2 (NIV).

played, young Croatians came to Jesus.

We arrived at the venue in Slavonski Brod and started to set up our equipment on an outdoor stage. Dark clouds lingered ominously, and we were nervous because the stage had no covering. We had a local band open the show, and they performed much longer than we had agreed upon (shocking, right?). While their set dragged on, the weather worsened.

With drops of rain beginning to come down, we started to play, and a large crowd gathered. Right at the point where we show the character of Jesus being crucified on stage, it started to rain harder. Soon it was torrential. The wind was blowing hard, and then the lightning and thunder began. I had no idea what to do. All our equipment was getting soaked, and we were totally exposed. I looked over at our bass player, and he seemed unaffected. He just stayed in character and kept playing as the rest of our band ran around in panic. Finally, the power simply shut off, and the show was over.

Stopping in the middle of the crucifixion isn't exactly ideal when presenting the gospel. Undeterred, David jumped off the stage and, with the rain pouring down, shouted, "If you want to know Jesus, I want you to kneel in the mud with me right now!"

Over thirty people knelt and prayed out loud. One simple sentence was all God needed to change lives!

I learned that night that although God chooses to use our gifts, he doesn't need them, and this is a good thing. If the fruitfulness of my ministry depended on the quality of my performance, the pressure would be unbearable and the results unimpressive. Thankfully, God produces the change, and on this particular night, he did so at our weakest moment to demonstrate his great strength.

Throughout the years, he has continued to reinforce this reality.

One time we played in Lagos, Portugal, and it was clear from the beginning it would be a challenge.

About thirty minutes before we were supposed to perform, the city official who had signed the permit for us to play threatened to cancel the show. She claimed she had no idea that we were a rock band and would be playing loud music.

My brother Aaron and I gathered with our local promoter, and we prayed for wisdom. Almost instantly I felt that we should offer a shortened version of our show as a compromise, and Aaron felt the same thing. Denny, our regional organizer, pitched the idea, and the city official agreed. I wasn't surprised. God had spoken clearly, and I knew that he would soften her heart.

We frantically started the show, but the challenges continued. The city official persisted, harassing our sound guy. Between every song, she would ask, "Is it over yet? Turn down the volume!" He fought her off as best he could, but by the end of the show, we barely had any sound coming through the speakers.

A crowd of around four hundred people had gathered to watch us play, including a group of about fifty rowdy teenagers at the front of the stage, who were dancing and yelling.

I wasn't sure how these people were going to receive the gospel. We had to play a shortened version of our show, the sound was almost turned off, and all circumstances seemed turned against us—but when Aaron started to preach, God's power fell. Instead of laughing and mocking, the crowd listened quietly. When my brother asked for a response, many people raised their hands, including several of the rowdy teenagers.

We talked to Glen, a young guy from Belgium, who thanked us for playing. He said that at his school they were taught that God is dead. Yet, after our show, he said he felt "complete" for the first time in his life, and he prayed with Aaron to receive Jesus!

Despite the adverse circumstances, many lives were changed that night.

God is not impressed or limited by human circumstances. He doesn't need a perfect venue or a great show. We have been reminded over and over again that there is power in the gospel and that if we are willing to lift up the cross in secular places, people will respond.

For fear of completely undermining the key argument of this chapter, let me be clear again: I believe in apologetics. But there is power that is exclusive to the message of the cross and cannot be found in rational arguments and persuasive words.

Sooner or later you need to get to the gospel. Results are not guaranteed, but people aren't products. Ultimately, the outcome is in God's hands.

5) Be Gentle and Respectful

In all our efforts to reach people for Jesus, we must act gently and with respect. This is incredibly important. Apologetics can help people see the cross or drive them far from it. We need to be delicate as we challenge the views of others, because, as Francis Schaeffer reminds us, doing so in a violent way "bereaves people of what shelter they have enjoyed heretofore."[97]

In defending the faith, we have to take every precaution to treat the person we are speaking with as a precious child of God.

Growing up, my mom would always remind me that it was useless to win the argument and lose the friend. I would roll my eyes, but as an arrogant young guy, this was exactly what I needed to hear.

People are not projects; they bear the image of God and have incredible worth. If our attempts to reach people are not fueled by God's power and motivated by his love, not only will they fail to produce fruit, but they also will cause great damage.

Paul says in 1 Corinthians 13:1, "If I speak in the tongues of men or angels, but do not have love, I am only a resounding gong or a clanging cymbal" (NIV).

Sadly, too much of Christian apologetics today is a "clanging cymbal." I have been guilty of this and have won arguments and lost friends. By God's grace, I have grown up and have seen

---

97   Francis A. Schaeffer, *The God Who Is There* (Westmont, IL: InterVarsity Press, 1968), 127–30.

God work powerfully through my use of apologetics to lead people to the cross.

Let It Be Clear!

I was invited to be the evangelistic speaker at a high school event with hundreds of unreached young people in attendance. I worked hard to prepare a message that would be relevant to a secular crowd, and I prayed that God would move in power. When I arrived, I was told that there would be several speakers and various performances before it was my turn to speak. This didn't bother me until the program began. For nearly an hour, "Christianese" was on full display; long-winded testimonies were shared and a panel discussion took place in which the participants were asked to share their favorite Bible verses. I sank into my chair and couldn't help but think, "If I weren't a Christian, I would be long gone!"

I wondered whether I should change my message, but I ultimately felt that if even a handful of truly secular young people remained, I would speak to them.

Sadly, situations such as this are common. As Christians, we have become so out of touch with secular culture that we don't know how to reach people—and this is evident in our overly "churchy" outreach events.

Relevance is a complicated subject. It's multifaceted and, if misunderstood, can cause as much harm as good. Becoming relevant is about communicating the gospel clearly, unobscured by "church language" or out-of-touch methodology. No one was more relevant than Jesus. He spoke straight to the heart with striking power and clarity and was able to do so because he knew the people he was addressing.

Being relevant is about showing people who Jesus is. It means finding ways to present the real Jesus to a world that long ago rejected the one of its own making. It means living a life that reflects the transforming power at work inside you. Friedrich Nietzsche said, "I will believe in the Redeemer when the Christian looks a little more redeemed."[98] It isn't right that the lives of Christians often look strikingly similar to the lives of those who claim no religion at all.

Our actions and attitudes have incredible power. They can show people the heart and character of Jesus. We need to take seriously the task of becoming more like Christ for the sake of a world that's watching closely.

Relevance means engaging a secular world with effective presuppositional apologetics. We need to understand the secular mindset, highlight the coherence of the Christian faith, and patiently address people's objections to belief in God.

---

98   Strobel, *The Case for Faith*, 150.

7

THE POWER OF THE CROSS

Several years ago, I was part of a Christian battle of the bands. This was a popular competition in our city, and many of the winners went on to have national success.

As part of the scoring, we were required to give a message. I sat in the audience, waiting for our time to play, watching one of the bands perform. They ended one of their songs, and the lead singer said, "Our band believes love is the most important thing—so we do our best to love each other, and we want to try to love you." That was the end of his message.

I remember thinking, "That's nice, but that's not the gospel."

To be fair, the singer might not have intended to share the gospel, but as I sat there listening, I was struck by how rare it is to hear Christian artists talk about Jesus in a clear way. Many bands played that night and shared great testimonies and inspirational stories, but not one band talked about the cross.

The unwillingness to share the gospel is a growing trend in the Christian community today.

Just a few years ago, No Longer Music was playing at a Christian festival in New Zealand. On the last night, we decided to watch the headliner—a band that was arguably the most famous Christian band in the world at the time.

Throughout the two-hour performance, the singer said a lot

of things. He talked about love, encouraged us to care about the world, and at one point shared a story about how the band had overcome some tough times, but he said nothing about Jesus or the cross.

It's not just Christian artists who aren't sharing the gospel, but Christians in general. You don't hear it anymore. The consequence of our silence is great because without the resurrection, there is no power. I have personally experienced that when you are willing to share the gospel outside the church, God moves and people are changed. And yet sharing the cross is unpopular today.

My dad was invited to speak to a group of non-Christian young people at a skate park in New Zealand. Beforehand, the Christian promoter told him that he would prefer if he gave a "positive message" rather than an evangelistic one. My dad was dumbfounded by this bizarre dichotomy.

Strange as it may be, this is how many Christians view the gospel today. They might not use the word "negative," but they see the gospel as too intense, fundamental, or old school. The subtle perception among many Christians is that the cross is an old story and not appropriate for our modern times.

This mentality has paved the way for a Christian culture that will talk about anything but Jesus. We like to emphasize stories of life transformation or inspirational testimonies. We love to hear about alcoholics or drug addicts who came to Jesus and are now free of their addictions.

Hear me clearly: when you surrender your life to Jesus, he changes you; and when he does, we should celebrate that. But God is more than just another approach to behavior modification. A person can overcome addiction in many ways. Some go to therapy, some take medication, some try meditation, and some just rely on willpower and discipline. This idea may sound controversial, but Jesus is not the only one who can change your behavior. Thankfully, he does much more than that.

People do not need another self-help, life-improvement plan. They need to be made alive. They need to be reconciled to their Creator and forgiven for the bad things they've done. After all, Jesus did not come to make bad people good, but to make dead people alive. That's the difference between the gospel, and every other world religion.

Sadly, we have been selling people short by limiting Jesus to a program for behavioral change.

Paul says in Romans 10:14: "How then will they call on him in whom they have not believed? And how are they to believe in him of whom they have never heard? And how are they to hear without someone preaching?"

When Scripture so plainly instructs us to share the gospel, why are we remaining silent?

There are many reasons, but I will focus on five.

1) I Don't Believe It

Christians aren't sharing the gospel because they don't believe it's true. This might seem like a strange accusation, given that the cross is the essence of what it means to follow Jesus.

It all comes down to how you define belief. Authentic belief is something you act on.

A teacher of mine explained it this way: Suppose someone tells you that she owns a vault containing a million dollars. This person gives you the combination and permission to empty it. You may believe her, but of what value is this belief unless you take the money?

There are millions of people who claim to follow Jesus, and yet studies show that only a fraction of them ever share the gospel with the unsaved.[99] We have the cure for the world's deadliest disease, but so many of us don't share it. Given this, it's fair to ask: does our silence reveal unbelief? Without action, Christianity is just a nice idea—nothing more.

If I'm wrong and all Christians do believe in the gospel, then our silence is criminal. How can we believe that there is no other way to be saved from hell but through surrender to Jesus and yet not tell people about it?

Magician and atheist Penn Jillette (of Penn and Teller)

---

99   The Barna Group, "Sharing Faith Is Increasingly Optional to Christians," *Barna*, May 15, 2018, https://www.barna.com/research/sharing-faith-increasingly-optional-christians/.

famously said, "How much do you have to hate somebody to *not* proselytize? How much do you have to hate somebody to believe everlasting life is possible and not tell them that?"[100]

It's not enough to believe the gospel in our minds; it only becomes real when we live in light of its implications.

God continues to convict me in this area, and I daily need his mercy for times when my belief does not lead me to act. Ask God to give you a revelation of eternity, the cross, and the enormous implications of the choices we make. When he does, you will discover that there is a big difference between an idea in your mind and a belief that changes your life and the lives of those around you.

2) I Prefer Other Messages

Pursuing social justice is another popular substitute for preaching the gospel.

Social justice and the gospel were never meant to be distinct pursuits, and yet in Christian culture, there's often the perception that you either meet physical needs or spiritual ones.

I think this is a misunderstanding. We should feed the hungry and care for the sick—and doing this gives our preaching

---

100   Justin Taylor, "How Much Do You Have to Hate Somebody to *Not* Proselytize," *The Gospel Coalition*, November 18, 2009, https://www.thegospelcoalition.org/blogs/justin-taylor/how-much-do-you-have-to-hate-somebody-to-not-proselytize/.

authority—but they were never supposed to be mutually exclusive tasks.

I have a son. As a follower of Jesus, my first priority is his spiritual needs. But does that mean that I don't feed him when he's hungry, or buy him clothes when he needs them, or take him to the doctor when he's sick? I am deeply concerned about his physical needs. Would I be a loving father if I *only* gave him food and clothing but neglected his soul?

We are not called to live sheltered, indifferent lives, but instead to sacrifice ourselves in service to others. James tells us that pure religion requires us to "visit orphans and widows in their affliction."[101] Throughout history, followers of Jesus have been major forces for good and have devoted their lives to combating poverty, suffering, and inequality.

Some of the organizations started by Christians include the Red Cross, the Salvation Army, the Humane Society, Alcoholics Anonymous, World Vision, Amnesty International, and Habitat for Humanity, but without the truth of the gospel, these organizations would produce only temporary relief.

It is undeniable that God's heart breaks for the poor, the sick, and the marginalized. I understand the attraction to social justice and admire those who are making a difference, but being like Jesus means caring about the *whole* person without losing focus

---

101   James 1:27.

on the primacy of the soul.

Lasting change comes only from preaching the gospel.

If you want to end poverty, preach the gospel. Laws and programs cannot rid the human heart of greed, laziness, and selfishness, which are the greatest causes of socioeconomic disparity. Only Jesus can cure the underlying sin that produces evil and suffering in the world.

Do you want to end the sex trade? Preach the gospel. Only the power of God will cure the insatiable lust of our culture, which creates the demand that allows the sex trade to exist; only the power of God will awaken the apathy of those who should be fighting to end it.

Does your heart break for broken families? Preach the gospel. Only God's power can produce the self-sacrifice, humility, and grace necessary for families to thrive.

I am not trying to oversimplify the evil and suffering in our world today. Injustice and abuse are rampant, and we need to do something about it. But too often we focus on the symptoms and ignore the root causes.

There is no hope apart from Jesus.

Knowing what we know, how can we view a person's eternal fate as an optional concern? To neglect the gospel and focus on other messages is tantamount to providing a warm meal to someone in a burning building.

This is an appeal to *really* make a difference. To do so, we need to have an eternal perspective.

Jesus lived in a day of terrible social injustice. The Jews were being abused and oppressed by their Roman occupiers. The economic disparity was far greater than ours. The ruling elite controlled everything, and most people lived in poverty. Women were second-class citizens, and racism was ubiquitous.

Jesus could have focused on fighting the social injustice around him. Despite the expectations of the Israelites and his followers, he chose not to. The Jews expected a conquering Messiah, someone who would restore Israel to its former glory. This theory was widely known, even to the Romans.

When Jesus was delivered to Pilate, Pilate asked, "What have you done?" Jesus replied: "My kingdom is not of this world. If my kingdom were of this world, my servants would have been fighting, that I might not be delivered over to the Jews. But my kingdom is not from the world."[102]

Jesus had an eternal focus, and the way he lived reflected that.

In another famous incident, a notoriously "loose" woman barged into a house filled with the religious elite, including Jesus, and, ignoring all social convention, she poured a very expensive bottle of perfume all over Jesus's feet. The disciples rebuked her, saying, "This perfume could have been sold at a high price and the money given to the poor."[103]

---

102   John 18:35–36.

103   Matt. 26:8 (NIV).

Jesus responded in an unexpected way. He said: "Why are you bothering this woman? She has done a beautiful thing to me. The poor you will always have with you, but you will not always have me."[104]

This statement seems harsh. Why would Jesus say such a thing? Was he indifferent to the plight of the poor? Clearly not. Jesus fed the hungry and healed the sick. But even though he cared for people's physical needs, it was not his *greatest* concern.

Jesus didn't come to earth to help people live better lives, but to forgive sin, speak the truth, and offer salvation to anyone willing to repent and turn to him. Jesus came to lead lost sheep home. He emphasized this when he asked, "What good is it for someone to gain the whole world, yet forfeit their soul? Or what can anyone give in exchange for their soul?"[105]

Jesus asked this in the context of the high cost of following him, but it reveals something about his priorities. God created the world, and he created it good, but even good things on earth are trivial when compared to eternity with him.

3) I Don't Want to Cause Offense

Paul was not confused about the centrality of the cross. In Philippians 3:8 he writes: "Indeed, I count everything as loss because

---

104   Matt. 26:10–11 (NIV).

105   Mark 8:36–37 (NIV).

of the surpassing worth of knowing Christ Jesus my Lord. For his sake I have suffered the loss of all things and count them as rubbish, in order that I may gain Christ."

Paul's commitment to the gospel was relentless, and it cost him his life. Why? Because the cross is offensive. It has been since the very beginning. The unwillingness to offend is a major reason why few Christians openly share the gospel today.

Paul reminds us of this fact in 1 Corinthians 1:23 when he says, "But we preach Christ crucified, a stumbling block to Jews and folly to Gentiles."

Jesus's death and resurrection was a major problem for the Jews. They expected a conquering king, not a dying savior. Interestingly, Paul's choice of phrasing, "Christ crucified," emphasizes this clash of expectations and reality. The word "Christ" is synonymous with the Hebrew word "Messiah," which means "anointed." "Messiah" was a title of reverence and honor. To couple "Christ" with "crucified" was a highly problematic paradox for the Jews. As Albert Barnes notes, "The Jews would make the Messiah whom they expected no less an object of glorifying than the apostles, but they spurned the doctrine that He was to be crucified."[106]

Paul calls the cross a "stumbling block" for Jews. For them, it would be hard to imagine a more offensive way for God

---

106   Albert Barnes, *Notes, Explanatory and Practical, on the First Epistle of Paul to the Corinthians* (New York: Harper & Brothers, 1858), 31.

to redeem humanity than his sending his son to die. For the Romans, even the rumor of a potential threat to their sovereign rule was offensive enough to take action, and ultimately Pilate submitted to the will of the mob and allowed them to kill Jesus.

It's important to understand that the cross has always been offensive, not just to our culture or during this particular time in history. Accepting this fact will allow us to preach the gospel knowing that causing offense is simply part of the deal.

The cross will always be offensive because it confronts our deepest idols and exposes our most entrenched rebellion against God.

The world says we should live to fulfill our needs, but the cross requires total self-denial. Jesus took all the punishment we deserve, doing for us what we could never do for ourselves. In Christ, there is no room for self-righteousness, because grace is a gift we can never earn. Taking hold of Jesus means giving up control, rejecting all other religions, and living entirely out of step with the dominant philosophies of secular culture today. Without exception, we must reject self-worship, relativism, universalism, and materialism, among many tenets of secular humanism, if we are to surrender to God.

Many Christians focus on messages other than the gospel because they have given in to the pressure of secular culture.

As I mentioned in the first chapter, our secular world has produced an intolerant version of tolerance that has been weaponized and aimed at absolute truth and at Christianity.

Tolerance when properly understood is an admirable thing. We have made considerable societal advancements under the banner of tolerance (such as improved gender equality and race relations)—and that's great. But tolerance generally is misunderstood and less benevolently motivated than it would first appear. The modern notion of tolerance is the guard dog of the secular perspective and has been used to bully anyone with differing views.

My belief is that our modern notion of tolerance is really self-worship. The right to self-determination seems hardwired into the modern mind, and it fuels our drive to promote tolerance. We resent anyone who tries to impose his or her views on us. Moral autonomy is the real heartbeat of tolerance.

Perhaps without realizing it, many Christians have succumbed to this "pattern of the world." We applaud absolute truth as a spiritual theory but vehemently oppose any judgments made against our ethical choices.

We have Christianized secular relativism and adopted the motto "That's between God and me" to replace the more secular motto "Don't tell me how to live!" In light of this, it's not a surprise that the gospel has disappeared from our sermons, our books, and our art. But Jesus said: "I am the way, and the truth, and the life. No one comes to the Father except through me."[107]

As followers of Jesus, we must embrace the offensiveness of

---

107   John 14:6 (NIV).

the gospel, because it is the truth. Our desire to see people saved must outweigh our unwillingness to offend. This idea is evident in our human relationships. A healthy friendship will include sharing hard truth. If I believe that my wife's behavior is destructive, I will tell her, even if it causes offense—because I care, and choosing not to intervene isn't loving; it's selfish.

In the same way, a genuine love for those who don't know Jesus will compel us to share the truth, no matter the cost.

4) I Don't Want to Look Foolish

We live in the most image-conscious era in history. We obsess over our physical appearances, our social statuses, and our reputations. This is certainly true of young people, but do we ever outgrow our need to be cool?

As adults, our image-consciousness becomes more subtle (no longer a matter of who has the coolest shoes) but no less consuming. We instinctively avoid anything that would hurt our image. We are tirelessly self-aware in social settings. We want to be friendly, but not creepy; make eye contact, but not too much; smile, but not excessively; be funny, but not obnoxious; informed, but not a know-it-all. Trying to be liked is exhausting.

Social media has exacerbated the problem. We are now defined by likes and followers, and our online presence requires constant maintenance.

It's no surprise that, given our image-conscious culture, Christians aren't talking about Jesus, because they think doing so is uncool. I know this is true because I am often guilty of the same thing.

In Romans 1:16, Paul declares, "For I am not ashamed of the gospel, for it is the power of God for salvation to everyone who believes, to the Jew first and also to the Greek." Pride has always been a barrier to sharing the gospel.

Paul was unashamed because he understood that the gospel had the power to accomplish the most significant task on earth: to save sinners.

This must be our focus as well. Self-consciousness is just self-ishness. God's heart breaks for those who don't know him, and he calls us to share the truth. If you find yourself immobilized by the fear of looking foolish, ask God to break your heart. I believe he will answer this kind of prayer and liberate you from the oppression of self-focus.

5) It's Hard

I have a friend, Justin, who has an unusual approach to enduring hardship. We were on tour together for a few years, and on the road, you tend to experience extremes. We were often exhausted, hot, and stressed out, and in the middle of these times he would get a wild look in his eyes, frantically rub his hands together, and yell out, "Embrace it! Want more of it!"

We would be in the Middle East during the summer, setting up our equipment in the heat of the day, and Justin would be jogging on the spot, "embracing" the heat. Beyond great comic relief, his attitude in dealing with difficulty taught me a lot.

Accomplishing something significant requires embracing difficulty because good and hard always go together.

As Christians, our goal is to live like Jesus, but when it comes to evangelism, so few of us are following his example. A Barna study concluded the following: "Only half (52%) of born again Christians say they actually did share the Gospel at least once this past year to someone with different beliefs."[108]

Why is this?

Put simply, "It's hard."

It's human nature to take the path of least resistance, so naturally, if given a choice between fighting for social justice or preaching the gospel, we rarely choose the latter. And why would we, when meeting people's practical needs is universally praised? We may disagree over the cause of or the solution to evil, but we applaud anyone who devotes their lives to helping others. To my knowledge, no one has ever been mocked, ridiculed, or rejected for feeding the homeless. On the other hand, preaching the gospel will bring you no such praise. In fact, when you talk about Jesus, you will face considerable opposition.

Our world is hostile to any absolute truth, let alone the exclusive claims of Christ. Additionally, we have an active enemy

---

108   The Barna Group, "Is Evangelism Going Out Of Style?" *Barna*, December 17, 2013, https://www.barna.com/research/is-evangelism-going-out-of-style/.

who loves nothing more than to keep us quiet. When you add to that our reluctance to offend or look foolish, it's no surprise that few Christians share the gospel today.

We have a motto in my family: "Good and hard always go together." I heard this all the time growing up. Maybe this doesn't seem like a revolutionary thought, but this simple concept has had an enormous impact on my life. I don't avoid hard things but instead, see them as part of accomplishing something significant.

I was driving one day and a commercial came on the radio. The product's slogan was "One more step towards pain-free living." I remember thinking, "There has to be more to life than that."

When I look at the things in my life that I value—being a husband and dad, going to many places to preach the gospel, and even writing this book—I see that none of them have been easy.

The 2016 No Longer Music tour of Ukraine was incredibly hard. Our mobile-stage trailer broke down, we had to send our drummer home with two broken teeth, and one of our actors developed a life-threatening infection.

Despite these difficulties, we were able to preach the gospel to thousands of people. We saw God's power radically transform lives, and hundreds prayed to receive Jesus. This tour was beyond good, and yet it also hit a totally new level of hard.

As followers of Jesus, we need to reject the spirit of our age that says, "If it doesn't come easily, it can't be right." We were not created for leisure; we were created for battle. This is true in terms of life in general, but even more so in terms of spiritual things. We have an active enemy who strongly opposes those who want to use their lives to further God's kingdom.

God calls his followers to share the truth. I promise it won't be easy. You will face opposition. It will require great courage, and it will involve risk. It will cost you your reputation, time, and energy, and maybe even your life. But there is no greater privilege than seeing God change lives.

Our world is a desperate place, and while you may have an easy life, most of the world does not. God has prepared you for good works to do in advance.[109] Jesus says, "The harvest is plentiful, but the workers are few."[110] I believe this is because of the cost of following Jesus in a radical way. Our flesh shrinks back from anything hard, and when things become a struggle, most people quit.

I think most followers of Jesus, if they are honest with themselves, know that they aren't sharing their faith enough. This is a source of guilt and shame for many, and this chapter is not intended to add to those feelings.

Remember: "There is now no condemnation for those who are in Christ Jesus."[111]

---

109   Eph. 2:10.

110   Luke 10:2.

111   Rom. 8:1 (NIV).

Following Jesus is not about what you do or do not do—that's religion. Jesus loves you completely, and there is nothing you can do to change that. Still, his heart breaks for those who don't yet know him. He desires that none would perish, and he longs for the whole world to experience the same freedom, life, and forgiveness that you and I have. It is out of this heart that Jesus appeals to you and me to share the greatest news in all of history: the gospel.

It Will Be a Fight

As we attempt to share the message of the cross, it's important to realize that we enter a battle; but this fight extends beyond our five senses. Paul reminds us that "our struggle is not against flesh and blood, but against the rulers, against the authorities, against the powers of this dark world and against the spiritual forces of evil in the heavenly realms."[112]

Satan and demons conspire with our flesh to kill, steal, and destroy. It's very easy to forget this. We can become so consumed with what is right in front of us that we forget the spiritual reality all around us. Paul's reminder in Ephesians speaks directly to this human tendency.

To fight effectively, we need a better understanding of spiritual warfare. Oddly enough, for many Christians, Hollywood's

---

112   Eph. 6:12 (NIV).

depiction of demonic activity is more influential than Scripture.

An in-depth study of spiritual warfare is beyond the scope of this book, but it is worth briefly examining. Satan is described as the father of lies in John 8:44, and I believe deception is his most effective weapon. It is certainly possible for spiritual warfare to manifest itself in more dramatic ways, but what a lie may lack in drama, it does not in power.

Try sharing your faith, and watch the lies come flooding in:

- You don't want to tell people about Jesus; you will lose your credibility.
- People don't need this as much as you think they do.
- If you don't say anything, then you will be able to have a greater influence in the future.
- You don't need to use words; just be a good person—that's enough.

How do we overcome these lies? In two main ways. First, by expecting them. Paul ends his first letter to the Corinthians by urging them to "be watching" and to "stand firm."[113] Paul knew that if they were to live out the calling God had placed on their lives, they were in for a fight, so being prepared was critical. If you know that you are in a battle, everything changes.

---

113   1 Cor. 16:13.

As a soldier, you are not surprised by obstacles or opposition. A civilian turns back at the first sign of difficulty, but a soldier anticipates it.

The other way we fight against the lies of the enemy is with the truth. Paul says we overcome being conformed to the world's patterns by the renewing of our minds.[114]

We must daily renew our minds with the truth, which is found in the Bible. Paul reminds Timothy that "all Scripture is breathed out by God and profitable for teaching, for reproof, for correction, and for training in righteousness, that the man of God may be complete, equipped for every good work."[115]

As followers of Jesus, we will not survive if we are not intimately aware of God's Word. Consider the beautiful imagery found in Proverbs 6:20–23:

> My son, keep your father's command
> and do not forsake your mother's teaching.
> Bind them always on your heart;
> fasten them around your neck.
> When you walk, they will guide you;
> when you sleep, they will watch over you;
> when you awake, they will speak to you.

---

114   Rom. 12:2.

115   2 Tim. 3:16–17.

For this command is a lamp,

this teaching is a light,

and correction and instruction

are the way to life (NIV).

The truth is our only weapon in the fight against our enemy. Satan will try to convince you that you don't need to talk about Jesus because there are many ways to be saved. But we know that's a lie because Jesus said: "I am the way, and the truth, and the life. No one comes to the Father except through me."[116]

Our enemy will try to tell you that your salvation depends on your good deeds. But we know this is untrue because Paul says clearly in Ephesians 2:8–9, "For it is by grace you have been saved, through faith—and this is not from yourselves, it is the gift of God—not by works, so that no one can boast".

Our enemy will try to convince you that you are unworthy to be used by God. But Paul reminds us that "God chose what is foolish in the world to shame the wise; God chose what is weak in the world to shame the strong."[117]

If we are going to reach the secular world for Jesus, we need to be prepared to fight. What's more, we need to know what kind of fight it's going to be and how we can win. Our struggle

---

116   John 14:6 (NIV).

117   1 Cor. 1:27.

is against an enemy whose primary weapon is lies—so only by knowing the truth can we prevail.

My dad has always said, "Where there is no cross, there is no power." This principle has guided him for over thirty years, as he has preached the gospel to hundreds of thousands of people. His approach has changed over time, but the commitment to preaching Christ and him crucified has never changed.

As an artist, I have made a commitment to share Jesus from the stage. It hasn't always been easy, but I have seen incredible life transformation. God has called all of us to reach the secular world for Jesus, but only through his power will we be fruitful, and this power only comes when we talk about the cross.

8
COURAGE

The Bible is not a collection of human-made myths or a book of moral rules; it's God's revealing himself to us. A friend of mine once said, "Don't just read the Bible—let it read you." For a long time, I thought Scripture was unique only in the sense that it's true.

This is certainly the case, but it is far more than that. God speaks specifically to each one of his followers through the Bible.

For years, I would read Scripture without ever letting it "read me." It had become little more than a religious routine and had very little impact on my life.

In time, I learned to read Scripture expecting to hear God's voice, and it changed my life. One of the more powerful examples of God's speaking to me through Scripture happened during a recent reading of Nehemiah. This experience had such a profound effect on me that it has largely guided the structure of this book.

Nehemiah modeled a high view of God, desperation in prayer, and a broken heart for the needs of the world. Perhaps the thing that struck me most was Nehemiah's courage. The first chapter of Nehemiah ends with a critical verse: "'O Lord, let your ear be attentive to the prayer of your servant, and to the prayer of your servants who delight to fear your name, and give success to your servant today, and grant him mercy in the sight of this man.' Now I was cupbearer to the king."[118]

Nehemiah had a prestigious job: he was a royal cupbearer. He tested the food and wine of the king to safeguard against assassination attempts. To our modern minds, this might not seem like a great job, but it was. It meant that the most powerful man in the world trusted Nehemiah with his life. As a royal official, Nehemiah enjoyed the security, wealth, and power that came with being a high-ranking aristocrat.

In a time when most Jews were suffering, Nehemiah had a great life, but he also had a lot to lose. He had his future and family to consider. Stepping out and asking the king for help would mean risking everything he had, even his life. To do nothing would have been reasonable.

It's easy to forget that this isn't a fictional story but a historical event. We can be guilty of reading biblical stories with the end in mind. Thanks to Hollywood, even the nonreligious know that the lions didn't eat Daniel, and that Joseph became a prince, and that Jesus rose from the dead. But for secular culture, these are merely stories and not real-life accounts.

We can make the same mistake with Nehemiah. We know things work out well, so we can minimize the tremendous courage Nehemiah needed to risk it all.

---

118   Neh. 1:11

My prayer is that God has used this book both to challenge you and to inspire you to act. What I have learned is that you can understand the need, respond in desperate prayer, even have a broken heart for the lost, but still do nothing because you're afraid.

It is for that reason that I choose to end this book by talking about courage.

Prayer is the fuel, a broken heart is the right motivation, but it is courage that moves you to act.

What Is Courage?

To have courage, we need to know what it is, and most people don't. It's never arbitrary but is always based on something.

I have boldness in a fight because I believe that I am stronger than my opponent. I have the courage to stand in front of strangers and speak because I am confident that the audience will appreciate what I have to say. So often, God stirs our hearts and we feel compelled to act, but we lack the courage to follow through. Why? It's likely that our courage is based on the wrong thing.

Maybe we weigh the problem against our talents or resources and think, "This isn't adding up; I don't have what it takes." Or maybe we focus on our struggles and decide, "I'm too weak and too sinful; there's no way God can use me."

In both cases, the problem is that we are looking to ourselves. We are no match for the problems in the world today. They are too big; we are too small. They are too complex; we lack wisdom. Our courage cannot depend on what we have or do not have. If it does, we will shrink back and do nothing.

Real courage comes from looking to God.

For a time, our family lived on the edge of the red-light district in Amsterdam. My parents had to remind my brother and me not to pick up the needles on the side of the street. As we walked home from school, we would have to avoid heroin addicts passed out on the sidewalks.

One day, rival gangs were fighting on the street just below our apartment building. One police officer showed up and, without hesitating, charged into the middle of the brawl. Immediately, the two sets of armed gangsters froze, dropped their weapons, and took off down the street. This was a strange scene, one cop chasing down a mob. After pursuing them for a hundred feet or so, he quickly turned around and ran back to his car, presumably to call for backup. It was as if it finally dawned on him: "I am very outnumbered!"

This bizarre scene illustrated a critical principle of courage. This officer so believed in the authority of the police force that he was willing to run alone into the middle of great danger. Similarly, understanding God's authority over all things gives us the courage to respond to whatever he is calling us to.

Go back to the beginning of Hebrews 11:6. It says that we must believe that God exists.

Until we do, we will never have the courage to play our part in reaching the secular world for Jesus.

An academic understanding of God will not hold up in the face of difficult circumstances. Actual evidence of a person's faith in God is his or her willingness to act on that belief. We can't always see or feel God, but are we willing to act anyway?

Believing God exists means that we have the courage to act in all circumstances. If we are going to make a difference for Jesus, we need this kind of courage.

Courage Is Not a Feeling

Have you ever felt courageous one second only to lose heart the next? This happens when our courage is based on feelings, which are unstable, vulnerable, and don't always reflect reality.

Have you ever met a person who is sad even though everything around him is fine? Or the person who is happy even when everything is falling apart? Emotions are unreliable and a poor reflection of what is true. They are part of the human experience and are not inherently wrong—they just shouldn't be in charge.

Courage is a *decision*. We must *choose* to be courageous, just as we must choose to be loving, patient, and disciplined. There are days when I feel like serving my wife, but most days I'd rather serve myself. For the sake of my marriage and out of a desire to obey God, I choose to ignore my feelings, and I *decide* to serve my wife whether or not I want to. In the same way, we must *decide* to act courageously.

Another misconception is that courage is about being reckless.

According to action movies, it's acting without thinking. That isn't courage; that is stupidity.

I have been in full-time ministry for over ten years, and I have experienced a lot of fear. What I have learned is that real courage is not the absence of fear, but rather, a willingness to do what is right despite the fear.

God has a unique plan for your life. He has equipped you in a special way, placed you in a particular context, and, if you are willing, he will use you to make a difference. I have experienced this truth in my life. God created me to share the gospel from a stage. I can look back throughout my life and see evidence of God preparing me for this particular "good work."

I am far from perfect and often fail, but, with very few exceptions, I have shared the gospel from every stage God has given me the privilege to perform on.

When I was a teenager, I was in a band with some of my best friends. We made the mistake of letting my dad name our band, so we were called Boy Chicken. To this day, I have no idea where the name came from or why we agreed to call ourselves that.

We played at a monthly outreach event that my parents organized. For a time, this event was a big deal, and hundreds of kids were coming. The event's popularity grew, and big bands were asking to play with us, but we were the headliners no matter what. In retrospect, the thought of making serious adult bands open for the teenage band fronted by the son of the organizer is pretty amusing.

Nepotism aside, these monthly outreaches were a tremendous learning experience, and I grew a lot. From the very beginning, I made the commitment to preach at every show—no matter what opportunities came my way.

My commitment was put to the test. We entered a national high school battle of the bands and progressed to the regional round. This was a pretty big deal, and we were excited. We would be competing with the best bands in the area for a chance to go to the national finals.

This was by far the most high-profile opportunity we had ever had. Would we share the gospel? If we chose to preach at an event like this, it could not only impact our chances of winning, but also hurt our reputations—and there are few things more important to teenagers.

The night came, and it was our turn to play. I was afraid, but I chose to be obedient. I remember the moment clearly. We finished our last song, appropriately named "I Will Never Deny You," and in front of a large crowd and nationally famous judges, I told everyone that Jesus died for them and that they could be saved only through him.

We didn't qualify for nationals, but this was a critical test, and I believe I passed.

Since then, I have preached on many stages in many places, and I'm confident that it is what I was put on earth to do. I wish I could say that I overcame fear back in high school and never dealt with it again, but it wouldn't be the truth. Courage is like a muscle: for it to stay strong, you have to keep using it.

A few years ago, I was leading a Bible study in Minneapolis. In a time of prayer, God challenged me. So much of my ministry was focused on events; I felt that I needed to share the gospel without a stage.

I hated the idea. Most people think of me as a pure extrovert, but I'm not. I'd rather speak in front of a thousand people than meet one new person. I am a "slow starter." In new social situations, I sit back for a while, and only once I'm comfortable do I begin to engage. This makes one-on-one evangelism the very opposite of what I'm comfortable with. I'm aware that almost everyone struggles to share the gospel. Still, some personalities are more suited to street evangelism, and mine is not one of them.

Nonetheless, I felt God clearly say, "Go, hit the streets, and tell people about me."

I proposed the idea to our Bible study group, and we agreed that this was something we needed to do. My lineage being what it is, I searched for an angle. My dad is an unusual guy, and rarely does he do things in a conventional way. For years he has used coffins as props in street evangelism. He may actually hold the record for the most time spent in a coffin by a living person.

Halloween was coming up, and we decided to leverage the season for our purposes. My friend Ge wore a pair of stilts, a bright LED mask, and a long robe. We hung a sign around his neck that said "Do you believe in ghosts?" and then headed to a popular street near the University of Minnesota.

Leading up to the event, I was stressed out and thought, "This will never work. No one will want to talk to us. The team is going to be so discouraged when this doesn't work." The day of the event, the weather wasn't looking good, and I thought, "Great! The perfect excuse."

I called up my friend Steve, thinking, "Surely, he'll agree that we should bail," and he did. "Good," I thought. "We don't have to do it. We gave it our best shot. The weather just didn't cooperate." But as soon as I hung up the phone, I knew I was wrong. To make matters worse, the weather improved, and I called Steve to tell him that we were back on.

We met up, made final preparations, prayed, and headed out. I braced myself for a humiliating "character-building experience." I figured we'd walk around for an hour or so, not find anyone to talk to, and head home. I was wrong. The second we arrived, people began lining up to speak with us. I was amazed. Despite the freezing weather, people were eager to talk. The team was spread out, and everyone was having great conversations. Our Halloween gimmick led to conversations about life, truth, and Jesus. It was incredible to see God move through our simple act of obedience and willingness to step through fear.

Unfortunately, the fear never goes away. The next time God asked me to step out of my comfort zone, the fear came flooding back, and once again I had to step through it.

To be courageous is to do something that frightens you.

Difference makers for Jesus are not fearless; they choose to obey despite being afraid. It's easy to forget, but many of the heroes of our faith experienced great fear.

The apostle Paul didn't hide it. He wrote in 1 Corinthians 2:3–5: "I came to you in weakness with great fear and trembling. My message and my preaching were not with wise and persuasive words, but with a demonstration of the Spirit's power, so that your faith might not rest on human wisdom, but on God's power" (NIV).

Paul, the world's greatest missionary, was so afraid that he was trembling. I've only trembled one time in my life, and it was during my very first public speech. I was thirteen years old and had just started high school in New Zealand. My English teacher announced that our first assignment would be to give a five-minute speech in front of the class. Having never experienced public speaking, I wasn't too worried. I chose my topic: the D-Day beach invasions. I filled out my cue cards and practiced a few times in my bedroom.

The day arrived. Seconds into the first speech of the day, it dawned on me what I was about to do. As my turn inched closer, my heart pounded, and I began sweating. I stepped up and gripped my cards. As I began speaking, my knees started to tremble, and then my hands, and then even my voice was shaking. At one point, I remember trying to steady my hands on the table in front of me, but it didn't help. This was an awful experience. But I survived, and speaking is now, ironically, part of what I do for a living.

Another instance of intense fear would come many years later, on a No Longer Music tour of Eastern Europe. I was sitting on the edge of a bed in a small apartment in Southeast Ukraine. My wife, Courtney, was on the phone with her mom reassuring her that it was safe for us to be going to Beirut, Lebanon (the last stop on our 2014 tour). What her mom didn't know (and still doesn't know) is that the location of the show the next day was only a few miles from a war zone. Just a week before we arrived, a major city bridge had been blown up by pro-Russian separatists.

I barely slept that night. I kept dreaming that we were being shot at and had to hide behind our stage. I was so afraid that my stomach hurt. Despite the significant risk, we resolved to play the show and preach, but it was not for lack of fear. I felt like Paul: I was afraid but chose to obey anyway.

Take More Risks

Having courage means being willing to take risks. There is a cost to following God. Jesus said in Matthew 16:24, "If anyone would come after me, let him deny himself and take up his cross and follow me."

It's hard to find a more countercultural statement today than "Deny yourself." We live in a world that has no interest in self-denial. We are told that if we don't fend for ourselves, no one will. It's shocking how unapologetically selfish our culture has become.

I once heard a psychologist on a radio interview say: "People think they should prioritize the needs of others; this is wrong. We need to care for ourselves first. Once *we* are fulfilled, then we will be able to care for the needs of others."

How unbelievably backward is this thinking? My selfish desires are limitless. If I waited to be fulfilled before serving others, the wait would be indefinite. But that's how Satan works. He takes what is true and turns it upside down. Following Jesus in our culture is a risk because it means rejecting the prevailing mindset of our day. It means going against the grain.

Are you willing to stand apart from the world?

Following Jesus means taking up your cross. This is a difficult command to understand because the cross has become a sanitized religious symbol, when in reality it was a tool for execution and represented suffering and death. It showed how serious sin is and the sacrifice that Jesus was willing to make to set us free. Taking up our cross is an invitation to join him in the ultimate act of self-denial and to suffer with him for the sake of the lost.

The cross-bearing life is a far cry from the Christian cliché "The safest place to be is in the center of God's will," but this slogan accurately describes the mindset driving the choices of most believers today.

The problem is that the safest place to be is *not* in the center of God's will. This mentality stems from the prosperity doctrine, the false notion that God's plan is for you to be healthy, wealthy, and prosperous. My dad calls this the "pleasure gospel." This is the conscious or subconscious belief that God will keep us happy as long as we try to live a moral life.

It differs from the prosperity doctrine only in that it's more subtle. Those influenced by the pleasure gospel are often unaware. They will say all the right things, but their actions reveal that they worship a vending machine. For them, following Jesus is not about surrender but about satisfying their desires. Needless to say, this false idea of God is incongruent with a gospel that calls us to risky behavior and unsafe places.

God calls us to obedience, not safety.

But this shouldn't be a surprise. Scripture clearly shows that following Jesus is not safe. Nearly all of his first disciples were executed in gruesome fashion, as were the apostle Paul and countless martyrs throughout history.

The world desperately needs to experience the love and power of God, and yet so few Christians are willing to step out to make a difference. I think this is the case in part because of the perception that our safety is more important to God than our obedience.

So why should I risk my safety?

Jesus said in Luke 17:33, "Whoever seeks to preserve his life will lose it, but whoever loses his life will keep it." We were not made for self-preservation; we were made to change the world. Following God could cost you everything, but there is no greater reward than seeing lives changed.

In 2006, God began to open the door for No Longer Music

to perform in Turkey—a country of over eighty million people and fewer than five thousand Christians.

I have to admit that for years, I thought it was impossible for a Western rock band to share the gospel in a Muslim country. Our tours of Turkey, Iraq, and Lebanon showed that there are no closed doors for Jesus. But that doesn't mean it's been easy.[119]

By 2011, we were in the middle of an intense tour of Turkey. We battled government bureaucracy and hostile crowds, as well as extreme heat. We often had to drive all day between cities. Our mode of transport was a small blue van with no air-conditioning, which we affectionately named "The Hot Box." I would dump entire bottles of water all over my body, completely soaking my shirt, and within ten minutes I would be dry. By the end of our long drives, we would be delirious from the heat.

After one particularly long drive, we arrived in Manavgat. This city has a population of just under three hundred thousand people, and there is no Christian church. A police escort met us at the entrance of the city and guided us to our housing for the night.

The next day we drove to the center of the city. A large banner hung on the back wall of the stage; it said, "Welcome to the Ramadan Festival." The city had scheduled No Longer Music

---

119   Go to www.steiger.org/hoperising to watch a forty-five-minute documentary that tells the story of how God opened a door and allowed us to share Jesus throughout the Middle East.

as the opening act of its Muslim holy month celebrations. Not surprisingly, our promoter was very concerned.

Our main ministry partner in Turkey is an American missionary named Wild Willy Wilson. He has been faithfully serving in Turkey for over thirty years and has been jailed twelve times for sharing the gospel. He was instrumental in showing us that it is possible to share Jesus in the Muslim world. But even Wilson looked alarmed; this was not a good sign.

He just shook his head and said, "I've never been in a situation like this." Our local Kurdish promoter strongly encouraged us not to say "Jesus." "Just say 'God,'" he said. "It will be less offensive."

This tour was unique because it was one of the few times that my brother, my dad, and I were all on the road together. Still unsure of what we should do, we took a walk and asked God for guidance.

As we prayed, I felt as if he said: "When will these people get another chance to hear about me? I brought you here to tell the truth!"

We do our best to be sensitive, and we avoid causing needless offense, but we all agreed that God wanted us to tell these people about him.

This was a Shadrach, Meshach, and Abednego moment. These godly men were faced with a choice: bow down before the golden image set up by King Nebuchadnezzar or be thrown into the fiery furnace.

In Daniel 3:16–18, they respond to this ultimatum with astonishing courage. "Shadrach, Meshach and Abednego replied to the king, 'O Nebuchadnezzar, we do not need to give you an answer concerning this matter. If it be so, our God whom we serve is able to deliver us from the furnace of blazing fire; and He will deliver us out of your hand, O king. But even if He does not, let it be known to you, O king, that we are not going to serve your gods or worship the golden image that you have set up'" (NASB).

It's easy to discount their courage knowing that God intervened, but I believe they expected to die. They knew God could save them, but they didn't know if he would. And still, they chose to obey. Our concert at the Ramadan festival felt like a similar situation. Would we bow down to our fear and deny Jesus, or would we be obedient no matter the cost?

We decided to preach.

A large crowd gathered, including city officials, politicians, and the local media. We performed our theatrical depiction of the life, death, and resurrection of Jesus. As the last note of the last song rang out, David clearly explained that Jesus is not a prophet but the son of God and that only *he* could save us. I remember bracing myself for a negative reaction, but instead, the crowd clapped and cheered.

Over one hundred people signed up, wanting to know about our message. The mayor joined us onstage and presented us with a bouquet of flowers, and we were able to give his son a

DVD further explaining the gospel. It was an amazing night.

God's power to open doors and change lives was on full display as we shared the gospel at a citywide Ramadan celebration. The fact that we survived the experience is remarkable enough, but to have been received so positively defies human logic.

God is not limited by barriers, and we get the privilege of experiencing this when we step out and take risks. By this, I don't mean chasing an adventure or thrill seeking. Believe me—I would have preferred to have just played our music, said nothing, and gone home. But real faith means taking steps without knowing how things will end up; when we do, God moves.

Jesus has a plan for your life, and it won't be easy. It will most certainly involve risk. But I am convinced that there is no greater life than one poured out in service to God for the sake of those who don't know him—regardless of the cost.

True courage is taking an academic truth about God and acting on it. It means believing that pleasing him is more important than personal comfort, popularity, or physical safety. In our case, it meant being willing to share the truth at the Ramadan festival in Turkey.

Admittedly, this experience was extreme and most likely more daunting than relatable. If you feel this way, it's understandable. It's important to know that being brave has less to do with one big decision and more to do with thousands of small ones.

It's about having a lifestyle of saying yes to God, taking one step of obedience after another. King David was able to face

Goliath only after he overcame the lion and the bear as a young shepherd. Don't worry about the courage you will need for a future fight; take the step in front of you, overcome fear, and watch your courage grow.

God can break your heart for the lost, you can drop to your knees in desperate prayer, but until you step through fear and act, you will produce no fruit.

Billy Graham said, "Believers, look up—take courage. The angels are nearer than you think."[120]

This simple statement reveals a lot about his understanding of courage. He knew that it was something we must "take" because it will never come to us automatically. What's more, he understood that the source of real courage is a profound awareness of God's power and authority over all things. By looking to him, we can have courage in all situations, because he is greater than anything we will ever face.

As Jesus reminds us in John 16:33: "In this world you will have tribulation. But take heart; I have overcome the world."

Jesus calls us to a life of risk. This is not for a few crazy people, but for all of us, especially those who want to reach the secular world for Jesus. Until we are willing to answer the call, I'm afraid

---

120   Billy Graham, *Angels* (Nashville, TN: W Publishing Group, 1975), 39.

we will live ordinary lives, and the world will go on unchanged.[121]

It's Time to Act!

When No Longer Music was touring recently with a famous secular band in Brazil called Medulla, our driver went into a lane not intended for the height of our bus. Traveling at well over sixty miles per hour, we smashed into a horizontal steel beam, which knocked our air-conditioning unit clean off and ripped a hole in the roof of the bus.

I have never experienced a more violent moment in my whole life.

Thankfully, no one was hurt, but we were shaken up and wondering what to do next. We were scheduled to host a follow-up meeting for those who had responded to the gospel at the show the night before.

Initially, we considered canceling, but David encouraged us to not let Satan win. Determined to make this meeting happen, we ordered a bunch of Ubers and made our way to the venue.

When we arrived, it was immediately apparent that this was not a typical spot for a follow-up event. In fact, the location was nothing like I'd imagined it would be. The band we were playing with guided us towards a large rock overlooking a Rio de Janeiro beach. Apparently, it was a famous spot where thousands of tourists and locals gathered to celebrate the sunset each night.

---

121   For a more in-depth look into taking risks for Jesus, check out www.onethousandrisks.com from Steiger missionary Chad Johnson.

We had been forced to unload all of our bags from the damaged bus, so, comically, we now had to drag our suitcases and backpacks several hundred feet up this rock. It was a ridiculous sight.

As the team and I made our way there, I still wasn't sure what the plan was. I asked our promoter, Moah, who replied: "Oh, it's simple. Medulla will play a few songs and then you'll preach."

A typical follow-up meeting is held in a cafe or church building for people who have responded to our message. This was clearly going to be anything but typical.

The band started to play, and a large crowd of people gathered on all sides. I was still rattled by the accident, and my skin burned from the fiberglass explosion we had experienced.

I thought: "God, this is not what I was expecting. Usually, when I preach, it's after a big show, with live music, lights, video, and special effects. I don't have any of my normal tools. How is this going to work?" I was feeling vulnerable and unprepared.

As Medulla's last song ended, I prayed: "Okay, God. I am so fragile, I have no control, and there is nothing about me that is impressive, but I will not let Satan win. You love these people and want them to know the truth. I may not have the support of a great show, but I believe you will work anyway!"

I took a deep breath and began to speak, and immediately I could feel God with me. I told the large crowd that they were not made to worship the sun, but the one who made it. I explained how they were not accidents, but were created by a God who loves them. I affirmed that they could be forgiven, healed, and set free. I then asked those who wanted to know Jesus to raise their hands and pray out loud. The crazy thing is, many of them did!

Heading to our housing that night, I was exhausted, but I felt totally content.

Are You Ready?

My dad and I often talk about how not all tiredness is the same. There is the kind that comes from simply not taking care of yourself—staying up too late, not eating healthy food, etc. Another kind comes from relying on your own strength instead of God's power.

But that night in Brazil I felt tired in a way that was deeply satisfying. It was an exhaustion that comes when you participate in the radical good works that God has prepared in advance for you to do.

You were created to be tired—the good tired. The kind that comes from pouring yourself out in the service of others. Only then are we truly filled. Your life was never supposed to be about joining a social club, living a moral life, and accumulating possessions, before finally growing old and dying. The Christian life was always supposed to be radical, countercultural, and world-changing.

You were created to reach the secular world for Jesus.

Are you ready?

My prayer is that you are ready to act—not haphazardly, but in the way that will lead to significant change.

Respond by seeking God. Pray like you've never prayed before. Let it disrupt your schedule. Ask for unreasonable things and demand that God move in power in and through your life, and don't stop asking until he does.

Respond by opening your eyes. The world is on fire. More than ever, people are hurting and need the truth. This should break your heart! Get to know people, ask them questions, and listen. As a pastor of mine once said, "Be free of the burden of always thinking about yourself."

Respond by leaving your assumptions at the door and learn the questions people are really asking. Help them see how believing in God is rationally sound, historically accurate, and philosophically congruent. Demonstrate that, unlike secular humanism, our faith is internally consistent and corresponds with how we really experience life.

Respond by stepping through fear, boldly preaching the cross, and taking Holy Spirit–inspired risks, and don't wait. We may feel as though we have all the time in the world, but we don't.

Paul reminds us in Ephesians 5:15–16, "Be very careful, then, how you live—not as unwise but as wise, making the most of every opportunity, because the days are evil" (NIV).

Don't waste your life. Time is short, and the needs are great. It's time to act!

STUDY GUIDE

Chapter 1
Understanding the Need

1. Reflect on the following statement: "There has never been a more unified youth culture than there is today." What impact does this have on your approach to reaching young people outside the church with the gospel?
2. Describe the impact the "three philosophical pillars" have had on your family, workplace, and neighborhood.
3. Look at the spectrum on page 5. Is this consistent with what you have experienced? Why or why not?
4. Do you believe that, if given the chance, secular young people will respond to the gospel? Why or why not?

Chapter 2
The Source of Power

1. Reflect on the following statement: "Real moves of God are built on prayer, not strategy." Do you agree with this? How might this conviction change the way you act in the future?
2. What comes to mind when you think of God? Reflect on

the idea that your view of God has a tremendous impact on your prayer life.

3. What are some desperate prayers God is asking you to pray?

4. When do you find yourself turning to prayer? What does that reveal about your view of seeking God?

5. "You are unique; your prayer life will be, too." What is unique about how you talk to God?

Chapter 3
The Motivation

1. Read Luke 15:3–7 and write down some attributes of the good shepherd.

2. Reflect on the following statement: "Before doing anything for God, you had better be clear about your motivation." Why is your motivation so important?

3. How do you view people who are outside the church? Is your heart broken for them?

4. After spending time in prayer, ask God to bring to mind people for whom you need a broken heart.

Chapter 4
Close the Gap. Speak the Right Language!

1. Assess your ability to communicate in the language of secular people. Have you become a foreigner in your own city?

2. Write down any "church language" that could be an impediment to someone's understanding your message.

3. Practice sharing the gospel out loud. Pay attention to any words or phrases that you use that would not make sense to someone with no church background. Rework your dialogue and try it again.

4. Are you living in a Christian ghetto? What are some specific steps you can take to get out, and how can you begin to implement them?

Chapter 5
Show Them Who Jesus Is

1. Reflect on the following statement: "Most unbelievers have an inaccurate perception of Jesus." Does this change your approach to evangelism? If so, how?

2. Reflect on the following statement: "Art can speak in a way that words simply cannot." Do you agree? Why or why not?

3. What are some creative ways that people without traditional artistic skills can use art to share Jesus?

4. Do you agree that "the world sees Christians taking plenty of moral stands, but it doesn't see us showing mercy enough. This perpetuates a false Jesus and leaves the lost in darkness"?

5. Examine your heart and ask God to reveal your attitude towards others. Do you show mercy as Jesus invites you to?

Chapter 6
Remove the Bushes That Obscure the Cross

1. What assumptions do you need to step back from to effectively engage the secular world?

2. Assess the role of apologetics in your interactions with non-Christians. Are you able to defend your faith and address barriers to belief in God? If not, what practical steps can you commit to taking in order to change that?

3. Read 1 Peter 3:15. Why is it important to "defend our hope"? What does Peter say about the kind of tone and attitude we should have in defending our hope?

Chapter 7
The Power of the Cross

1. Do you agree that "the unwillingness to share the gospel is a growing trend in the Christian community today"? If so, why do you think this is the case?
2. Reflect upon situations in which you have chosen not to share the gospel. What were the reasons for that?
3. What do you find most challenging about sharing the gospel?
4. Reflect on the following statement: "Where there is no cross, there is no power." What does this mean to you?

Chapter 8
Courage

1. Write down a definition of courage. Do you believe it lines up with the biblical definition of courage?
2. Do you agree that courage is a decision rather than a feeling? If so, why is that significant?
3. Write down a step of courage you believe God is asking you to take.
4. Do you feel ready to share Jesus with the secular world? Is there anything holding you back?

GET INVOLVED!

If God has used this book to inspire you, and you would like to go deeper, consider the following next steps.

Host a *Jesus in the Secular World* Seminar or Class

The content in this book began as teaching material for a class taught in churches in the USA. To inquire about hosting a JSW seminar or class in your church, small group, or school, go to www.steiger.org/jsw.

Provoke & Inspire Podcast

The *Provoke & Inspire* podcast is a weekly conversation featuring four Steiger missionaries (David Pierce, Chad Johnson, Luke Greenwood, and me). It is intended to challenge followers of Jesus to have radical faith in the secular culture.

The hour-long episodes include a mix of compelling illustrations, humor, and principles derived from decades of missional experience.

Go to www.comeandlive.com/podcast, or search for "Provoke & Inspire" on iTunes, and be sure to subscribe, rate, and review!

Steiger International

Steiger International is a rapidly growing worldwide mission organization that is called to reach and disciple the globalized youth culture for Jesus.

Steiger raises up missionaries and equips the local church to proclaim the message of Jesus in the language of the globalized youth culture and establishes long-term teams in cities through creative evangelism, relevant discipleship, and local church partnerships.

For more information on Steiger and how you can get involved, go to www.steiger.org.

Steiger Missions School

If you feel called to join Steiger International, the first step is to attend the Steiger Missions School (SMS). This school takes place twice a year at our International Center in Krögis, Germany, and lasts for ten weeks.

The SMS is intended for people with a wide variety of gifts and backgrounds who feel called to join Steiger's mission to reach and disciple the globalized youth culture for Jesus.

For more information and to apply for the missions school, go to www.steiger.org/sms.

Come&Live!

Come&Live! is a worldwide community of artists who are boldly using their God-given talents to share the revolutionary message of Jesus with those outside the church.

As such, our mission is to reach the globalized youth culture for Jesus by provoking and inspiring creatives of every style and genre to share the gospel with this mostly unreached generation through their art.

For more information on Come&Live! and how you can get involved, go to www.comeandlive.com.

No Longer Music

No Longer Music is an evangelistic music and theatrical production group that uses the stage to communicate the gospel of Jesus in nightclubs, city squares, and festivals to many thousands of young people every year who would never set foot in a church.

To learn more about No Longer Music, go to www.steiger.org/nlm.

ABOUT THE AUTHOR

Follow Ben on social media

Twitter: Twitter.com/benalanpierce

Instagram: Instagram.com/nzbenpierce

Ben Pierce is a member of the Steiger International Leadership Team and director of Come&Live!, a worldwide community of artists boldly using their God-given talents to communicate the revolutionary message of Jesus to those who have yet to hear it.

As the chief communicator for *Provoke & Inspire*, a popular weekly podcast, Ben writes articles and teaches seminars. He is passionate about challenging and equipping Christian artists to use their creative gifts to share the message of the gospel outside the church.

Ben speaks regularly at churches, conferences, universities, and seminaries around the globe. He challenges people to live lives of radical faith and to courageously engage the globalized youth culture with the gospel.

He teaches a specialized course called *Jesus in the Secular World*, which provides an in-depth understanding of the secular mindset and practical ways to relevantly engage a culture dominated by secularism and moral relativism.

Ben is also the lead singer and guitarist of No Longer Music, an evangelistic music and theatrical production group that uses the stage to communicate the gospel of Jesus in nightclubs, city squares, and festivals to young people who would never set foot in a church.

If you would like to inquire about inviting Ben to speak at an event, please send an email with specific details to usa@steiger.org.

ACKNOWLEDGMENTS

I want to thank my amazing family, Courtney, Macklin, Tayva, and Lenna. Without their patience and support, none of what I do would be possible.

I want to thank my parents, David and Jodi, whose lifework is the reason I am able to write at all.

I want to thank my brother, Aaron. Together, we shaped the material for *Jesus in the Secular World*, the class that would become the basis for this book. His support throughout the process has been instrumental in making this happen.

Shout-out to Steven Bradley and Jake "Big J" Jaderston for the many months of painstaking editing, laughter, and good times. This book is better because of you guys.

Thank you, Maureen, for your brilliant editing skills and tireless work ethic to make my writing better.

Thanks to Nicci J. Hubbert for your help in taking this book to another level.

I want to thank Wooddale Church, and specifically Richard Payne and Carol Buchanan, for supporting this project and helping make it a reality.

Thanks Derek Thornton and Cristian Faber for your incredible design work!